DISEMBODIED VOICES

DISEMBODIED VOICES

RODNEY DAVIES

ROBERT HALE · LONDON

© *Rodney Davies 2000*
First published in Great Britain 2000

ISBN 0 7090 6719 4

Robert Hale Limited
Clerkenwell House
Clerkenwell Green
London EC1R 0HT

2 4 6 8 10 9 7 5 3 1

Typeset in 11/13 pt Garamond by
Derek Doyle & Associates, Mold, Flintshire.
Printed in Great Britain by
St Edmundsbury Press Limited, Bury St Edmunds
and bound by
Woolnough Bookbinding Ltd.

Contents

Acknowledgements

I thank all those people who kindly took the time and trouble to write to me about their experience of hearing a disembodied voice, many of whom did so after hearing my late-night request for such information nationally broadcast on the James Whale Show on TalkSport Radio. Special thanks are extended to James for inviting me on to his programme, whose help in this regard has been invaluable and whose interest in the subject was most encouraging. My gratitude also goes to Mary Rose Barrington of the Society for Psychical Research, to Professor Judith Whitehead of Lethbridge University, Alberta, to Dr Kenneth Dodds, and to the staff at the British Library, where most of my historical research was done. I dedicate this book to them all.

The copyright material shown below is kindly reprinted by permission of the publishers. *British Medical Journal* 1997: 315; 1685–6. British Medical Publishing Group: *Diagnosis made by hallucinatory voices* by I.O. Azuonye. Faber & Faber Ltd: *Adventure in Search of a Creed* by F.C. Happold. Routledge: *Wine in the Ancient World* by Charles Seltman. However, despite every effort being made to contact all authors or publishers of copyright material, this proved impossible in some cases. My apologies are offered to those concerned.

List of Illustrations

pher, who once heard his mother, some seventy miles away, call out his name

10   Lord Herbert of Cherbury who, upon completing *De Veritate*, prayed to God for a sign of his approval and, to his delight, was given one immediately

11   St Benedict after he was saved from starvation by a priest who brought food to his lonely cave in response to an angry disembodied voice

12   Giovanni Bernadone (later St Francis of Assisi), who was spoken to by a disembodied voice while praying before a crucifix

Illustration Credits

Dan Slatter: 2. Dorothy Wratten: 3. Jean Akerman: 4. Jean Woodbridge: 5. Jeff Warlock: 6.

All other illustrations are from the author's collection.

1   The Disembodied Voice

> She looked north, and also south,
> And saw light come from out his mouth,
> That lay beside her in the bed. . . .
> And on his shoulder, golden red,
> She a cross beheld, and heard
> An angel speak with holy word.
>
> From *Havelock the Dane*

Disembodied voices are voices which are seemingly heard to come, usually singly, from out of thin air or which are experienced inwardly alongside that of ordinary consciousness. James Boswell, in his biography of Dr Samuel Johnson, records them being discussed at a dinner party given by the great man in April 1781, during which Dr Johnson revealed that when he was a student at Oxford he had once heard the voice of his mother, who was then some seventy miles away at Lichfield, in Staffordshire, call out his name. Boswell comments that such 'callings' are by no means rare and adds that they are 'as wonderful as any other mysterious fact, which many people are very slow to believe, or rather, indeed, reject with an obstinate contempt'.

Yet despite their seeming impossibility, hearing disembodied voices is surprisingly common – various surveys, for example, have found that about 5 per cent of the population have at one time or another been privy to them – although their study has long been hindered by their association with mental illness, notably with schizophrenia, which explains why they are seldom mentioned by those who have experienced them. After all, nobody wants to be thought of as not quite right in the head.

The hearing of such voices has a very long history, and indeed we have accounts of them dating back some four thousand years. Those familiar with the Bible will know that the voice of Jehovah was often heard by early Hebrew patriarchs like Moses and Isaiah, and that the Ten Commandments, which form the basis of Western morality, were dictated to Moses by Him. Similar divine directives also reputedly came from pagan deities, of whom the most notable in this regard is the Mesopotamian sun-god Shamash, who supposedly verbally imparted the earliest known code of laws to the Amorite monarch Hammurabi in about 1775 BC.

But hearing the voice of God or, more accurately, a heavenly voice, while being the most remarkable manifestation of this phenomenon, is not something that only occurred in the distant past. As we shall discover, many people in comparatively recent times have purportedly heard God speak to them, some of whom are alive today. And although the Deity may no longer give instructions of the same monumental importance as the Ten Commandments, His words have often had a profound effect on the lives of those so favoured.

Schizophrenics of course certainly do hear voices, which are a recognized symptom of the condition and which are considered to be hallucinatory by those treating them. These unwanted and distressing pronouncements are typically frequent and talkative, and what they say is usually negative in content, being accusatory, condemnatory or insulting to the hearer. The schizophrenic may be told, for example, that he is unworthy, dirty and disgusting, and as a consequence of this, he may sometimes be ordered to kill either himself or another person, whom the voice blames for his unpleasantness. To give itself a guise of unchallengeable authority, the voice may claim that it comes from the mouth of God, or it may purport to be that of the Devil or of one of his demonic cohorts. Sometimes too the sufferer may hear two or more voices conversing together about him in a similarly negative way. On

12

occasions, however, the voice or voices are uplifting and cheering in what they say, although such positivity is usually short-lived and is invariably followed by adverse criticism.

By contrast, the disembodied voices heard by mentally-normal people, which are the subject of this book, occur infrequently – perhaps only once or twice in a lifetime – and what is said by them is usually brief and is invariably helpful or informative. Sometimes the voice simply calls out the hearer's name, as happened to Dr Johnson, or alternatively that of another, or it may utter a sentence or two of advice or guidance, or a warning, or sometimes even a prophecy of things to come. When the voice is apparently that of God, the person addressed is seldom told who is speaking but either knows within himself or simply assumes that the source is divine.

I have heard an external disembodied voice on two occasions and can therefore testify to their reality and to their startling nature. On neither occasion was I in any way prepared for the sudden utterance, which added to the shock each gave me. The first, spoken by a voice I did not recognize, was advisory in nature, while the second, which belonged to someone I had known very well, seemingly came as a plea from the other world.

The first disembodied voice spoke to me late one Friday night when, as a 19-year-old student, I was returning home from the University jazz club. I had earlier that evening learned from the girl with whom I fancied myself in love that she did not want to get involved in a steady relationship with me. This seeming rejection of my affections followed hard on the heels of a school love affair which had also ended badly – the girl in question had forsaken me for another – and these two disappointments in love, along with earlier ones, had together left me feeling very upset and sorry for myself, and perplexed by the apparently contrary nature of the female heart.

Then, as I approached the crossroads on the otherwise deserted University Road, I was addressed by a voice from out of the air. As far as I could tell it came from a point about seven or eight feet above me, somewhat off to my right and positioned over the iron railings beside which I was walking. In a clear, audible manner it said, 'You don't have to fall in love with them.'

Absolutely astonished, I stopped and stared up. There was nothing above me except the dark sky. I spun around and looked back down the street, and saw that there was no one in sight who could possibly be the source of the voice. I gazed up again, trying to comprehend what had happened and feeling as awe-struck, I suppose, as Saul had when a voice from the air addressed him on the road to Damascus.

My astonishment was made even greater by the fact that what the voice said was truly revelatory. Until that moment I had believed that falling in love followed on naturally from meeting and dating an attractive girl. Yet the voice effectively told me that I could stop myself from being hurt by the opposite sex by controlling my feelings, by in other words not allowing myself to become so easily smitten by love. I had never imagined that such a thing was possible. But I understood immediately that I did not have to be swept helplessly along by my emotions and left vulnerable to future heartache and anguish. Rather, I could and perhaps should exert some control over them.

However, while I was totally stunned by what had happened, I did not think that Jesus or God had uttered those timely words, although I suppose I assumed that the voice had an otherworldly origin. As to its character, I recall that the voice was neither noticeably masculine nor feminine in tone, and that it had no accent. Indeed, I can only describe it as simply being a voice, which spoke matter-of-factly, much like any responsible adult with some knowledge of the world would when giving advice to a troubled young man.

The second disembodied voice addressed me, coincidentally enough, 19 years later. At the time I was in Greece, living alone in a rented house on the island of Ithaca. I had gone there with the intention of writing a novel, which I had decided to do following the death of my wife Maureen. She had died suddenly and unexpectedly five months before, and it was her voice that I heard.

The incident took place on the morning of 4 May of that year, when I woke up in bed. I was in fact roused from sleep by a strange shaking and shuddering within myself, which had happened to me several times before and which had once preceded an out-of-body experience. It often occurred when I fell asleep lying on my back, which was the position I found myself in that morning. Then, while still being shaken by the inner oscillation and half-way between sleep and full consciousness, I heard Maureen's unmistakable voice. It came from the other side of the sparsely furnished room, up where the wall met the ceiling and well above head height. It said: 'Help me'.

Moments later I was sitting up in bed, my heart racing, staring up at the place from where her voice had come. I believe I called out to her, but the opportunity for a dialogue had evidently gone as she said nothing else. The only sounds came from the birds outside. Maureen had therefore, or so it seemed, told me everything that she either could say or needed to say. But my shock at hearing her voice soon turned to puzzlement. Why, I wondered, did she need my help and how could I help her anyway?

I wrestled with these questions for some time, until at last I concluded that her spirit had for some reason not made the transition from this world to the next and that she had finally managed to get through to me audibly to say that she needed my assistance in this regard. And the only way I could do this, I realized, was through prayer, which is why, having dressed and eaten a hurried breakfast, I left the house and made my way to a small whitewashed church, which stood beside the narrow cobbled street leading up from the town. There I lit a candle for her and, kneeling before the altar, I prayed to God that she might be released from her unwanted sojourn here and helped into the next dimension of being. In this I believe I was successful, for I have never heard her voice again, despite often wishing that I could.

These two personal examples are representative of the fact that disembodied voices fall into two general categories, namely those that are recognized by the hearer and those that are not.

Where a recognizable voice is concerned, this may either belong to a living person or to someone who is dead. My experience of hearing my deceased wife's voice is of course an instance of the latter. When the voice is that of a living person, the words said are usually those then spoken by that individual, which implies that they are somehow able to manifest in the hearer's proximity, even though the speaker may be many tens or hundreds of miles away. And if there is survival after death, this is perhaps also true of the voice belonging to someone who is dead. Quite how this 'hearing at a distance' may occur is considered in a later chapter.

Yet many scientists and psychologists deny that such a thing can ever happen. Rather, they prefer to explain all disembodied voices heard by mentally-normal people as temporary hallucinations, induced by some trauma or upset, which causes the hearer to generate the voice within the hearing centres of his (or her) brain and who hears it as if it came from outside himself. Similarly, they maintain that when the words heard match those actually spoken at the time by that person, then it is merely coincidence.

But while the distressing and frequent voices heard by schizophrenics and other mentally-disturbed people may be nothing but hallucinations, such an origin cannot wholly account for the voices heard by sane people, for these often impart timely warnings and/or guidance which may preserve the hearer's life, or they may accurately predict the future.

Moreover, anonymous voices, as I can attest, often seem more mysterious, particularly when they are accompanied by an inner sense of the divine or if they possess a quality beyond that of the ordinary human voice. Where the latter are concerned, the voice heard by a man named J.D. Blackman is a striking example. Mr Blackman had been seriously ill for several weeks and, to add to his woes, had become increasingly depressed by his bedridden state, which brought him to such a low point that he stopped caring whether he lived or died. Then one night, to his intense surprise, he heard a voice speak to him.

'It was so close to my ear that I jerked my head away suddenly, and lost the words,' he informed the psychic researcher Hereward Carrington. 'The voice was a woman's voice – the clearest, purest, sweetest that a mortal being can conceive. No human voice could equal it in its qualities.'

The incident was made even more remarkable by the fact that Mr Blackman had the night before, while lying awake with the bedside light on, felt two large invisible fingers press his leg 'firmly, not hastily', just above the knee, which naturally startled him but at the same time made him aware that he had not taken his medicine. These ghostly fingers performed a similar warning function the night after he heard the voice, by again pressing his leg. And together, the disembodied voice and the touching fingers marked the turning point of his sickness, for Mr Blackman notes that 'from this time I began to mend'.

Such tactile impressions can be even more dramatic, to the extent that they may both accompany the disembodied voice and physically direct the person to whom the voice speaks. A good example of this joint action happened in December 1937 to Mrs E.E. West. One day while doing some washing she suddenly noticed that a ruby had fallen out of the gold ring she was wearing. Despite frantically searching for it, she soon gave it up for lost, assuming that it must have drained away with the water she had emptied from the sink. Yet next morning, when she was again in the kitchen, she heard a voice say to her, 'What about the ruby?', and before she realized that she was alone, she replied out loud, 'Oh, that's gone for good, it's no use troubling about that.'

Then, quite suddenly, Mrs West felt herself seemingly taken by the shoulders and turned around, whereupon she noticed the ruby lying on the floor, shining in a shaft of sunlight streaming in through the partially opened back door.

However, in her account of the experience published in the *Journal of the Society for Psychical Research*, she adds that 'I do not wish it to be thought that I felt my shoulders grasped, any more than I heard any particular person's voice, but that I was aware of myself as a person inside my body, but the same shape, which heard and felt quite well without my body.' This suggests that it was not Mrs West's physical self that was taken hold of but rather her double form, which resides, as readers of my book entitled *Doubles: The Enigma of the Second Self* will know, within the physical body.

We can only guess why Mrs West was helped in this remarkable way, but the fact that she was seemingly steered around towards the lost gemstone as if by invisible hands, does indicate that the incident was not caused by her previously becoming aware of the ruby at a subconscious level and thereafter generating the questioning voice herself in order to bring it to her conscious attention.

An even more striking instance of direct tactile aid is recounted by the celebrated goldsmith, sculptor and engraver Benvenuto Cellini (1500–1571) in his autobiography published in 1728. The event happened in May 1539 when Cellini was imprisoned, by order of Pope Paul III, in the notorious Castle of St Angelo at Rome, where he was placed in solitary confinement in a dark cell, whose floor was wet and which was home to numerous large spiders and other invertebrates. 'A wretched mattress of hemp was thrown down on the ground for me,' Cellini says, and his condition was made even more miserable by the fact that he had a broken leg. Hardly surprisingly, it was not long before the artist of genius became so depressed and despairing that, upon finding a heavy beam of wood in his cell, he 'poised it like a trap, intending it should fall on my head, which would certainly have crushed me to death on the spot'.

But just as Cellini was about to end his life in this rather bizarre fashion, he was 'seized by some invisible thing, and thrown four cubits' length from the place; and so terrified was I that I lay half dead; and there I stopped until the nineteenth

18

hour, when they brought me my dinner.'

Then a couple of months later, when Cellini thought he might be murdered by the castellan or castle keeper, he was addressed twice by a disembodied voice, which he believed belonged to the same guardian spirit that had earlier prevented him from committing suicide:

I could not see him, but he stood by me, lifted me up from the depths, and said in a clear voice, 'Ah, me! Benvenuto my friend, make haste. Assail God with thy wonted prayers, and cry aloud to Him!' Seized with sudden fright, I sank on my knees, and recited prayer after prayer in a loud voice, adding at the end the *Qui habitat in adjutorio*. Then I talked with God for a space. And all at once the firm, clear voice said, 'Go now and rest, and have no fear.'

Some years later, probably in 1543, when Cellini was living in Paris, where he had gone to work for King Francois I, a great admirer of his artistic talents, he heard another voice speak to him and again felt the touch of unseen hands. The incident likewise took place during a period of intense stress, which reached its peak when his model and lover Caterina unjustly accused him of having sodomized her, an offence punishable by death. When Cellini was summoned to court to answer the charge, he reluctantly decided to leave France and return to Italy. However, he then received some unexpected guidance.

Just as I rose to prepare for my departure, some invisible one took me by the shoulder and turned me about. Then a rousing voice said in my ear, 'Benvenuto, do as you are wont, and fear not!' On the spot I changed my mind entirely, and said to my Italian friends, 'Arm yourselves well, and come out with me, and do just as I bid you. Not another word on the matter, for I am going to answer my summons.'

The great artist was well advised by the voice, for he won the case, and he left the courtroom angrily shouting to the judge that both Caterina and her mother should be burned at the stake for their perjury. Fortunately, however, the judge demurred, and the wicked pair were sent on their way unharmed.

These two instances are both examples of the advisory disembodied voice, which speaks to recommend a particular course of action. A knowledge of the outcome is also implied, particularly in the second instance, as Cellini was entirely successful in defeating the slanderous charge made against him.

The following example of an advisory voice is perhaps even more astonishing, for it apparently gave a racing tip – and thus indirectly predicted the future – to a young man who had no knowledge of the horse mentioned or any interest in horse-racing or gambling. And yet he, by taking advantage of the tip, won himself a tidy sum of money.

The young man in question was Graeme Moore, the 22-year-old son of the writer and psychic researcher Margaret Gordon Moore, who fortunately preserved the incident in her book entitled *Coincidence – ?* Mrs Moore says that late one afternoon, when her son was rushing to catch a train home from London, he managed to buy an evening paper from a boy selling them on the platform. Indeed, it was this purchase which may have precipitated what followed. Then, having jumped into a carriage with the unopened paper in his hand, Graeme first put his hat on the hat rack. At that moment, his mother writes, 'he heard a clear resonant voice repeating "Bessamer, Bessamer, Bessamer," so clearly and loudly that he turned to see who was speaking so urgently.' Yet Graeme was startled to find that there was no one either behind him or indeed nearby, for the carriage was completely empty of passengers with the exception of himself. Hence the voice he had heard repeating the strange name had not emerged from a human throat.

On seating himself, the young man, who was familiar with the concept of spirit guides through his mother's interest in such matters, quickly concluded that he must have been addressed by one of them, although he had no idea why he had been. Yet the answer to this puzzle seemingly came shortly afterwards, when upon having opened his paper and read the city news, he turned quite by chance to the racing page, where, Mrs Moore records, 'the name Bessamer stood out as if in large capitals. It was the name of a horse, a rank outsider with tremendous odds against it, running the next day.'

This naturally led Graeme to suppose that Bessamer would win the race in question, which is why, on the following morning, he placed a to-win bet on it, and he was later gratified to learn that the horse, contrary all expectations (the odds against it were 100–6), had won. Yet while this may have been, as Mrs Moore points out, 'a very strange coincidence', she was entirely right to wonder 'but where did the voice come from in the empty carriage, pronouncing a perfectly unheard-of name repeatedly and urgently?'

Although such invisible spirit guides, if we may for the moment regard them as such, usually make their pronouncements spontaneously, they have throughout the ages been summoned to predict the future by sorcerers and magicians. Yet ironically, when conjured, the voice heard, like that of the deity which apparently spoke through the medium of the Pythia at the Greek shrine of Delphi, seldom gave a wholly unambiguous reply. And more bizarrely, among barbarian tribes in the Bronze Age, a decapitated human head was often used as a focus for the disembodied voice of its former inhabitant, who thereby spoke through it and who would, when consulted, prophesy the future. This prophetic function is ascribed in Greek myth to the decapitated head of Orpheus, the most talented musician and singer of antiquity. His head is not only said to have sung as it floated down the river Hebrus, wherein it was flung by the Maenads who had murdered and dismembered him, but on being carried by currents to the island of Lesbos, it was placed in an oracular cave at Antissa, where it regularly predicted the future, until silenced at last by order of the god Apollo. If there is any truth in this story, it was obviously not the physical head of Orpheus that spoke (which is impossible), but rather his disembodied spirit voice which declaimed the future through it.

Later on, a brass head was substituted for a real head, which apparently worked just as well, although the voice heard would normally have been unrecognizable to those who consulted it. This method of divination was popular in European countries until as late as the Middle Ages, albeit not without peril to those who practised it, for it was condemned by the Church as idolatrous and therefore evil.

However, because the spirits which spoke through brass heads were considered to be more knowledgeable of the future than human seers, the temptation to consult them sometimes proved too great even for high ranking members of the Church.

One story of a churchman, told by William of Newburgh (c. 1135–1200) in his *Historia Rerum Angliarum*, who had his hopes for the future unrealistically raised by a prophetic voice is worth repeating here, not least because the person concerned was the Pope. This was Sylvester II, formerly a Frankish bishop named Gerbert, who was born at Aurillac in Auvergne, in about AD 940, and who was made pontiff in April 999. He therefore held office at the end of the first millennium. Sylvester was a highly educated man, noted for his knowledge of chemistry, mathematics and philosophy, but who was also, like many in his day, fascinated by the occult arts. Indeed, three years after becoming Pope, Sylvester took it upon himself to consult a diviner employing a brazen head, of which he asked when he should die. The disembodied voice speaking through the head briefly replied, 'When it shall be your duty to celebrate the mass in Jerusalem.'

This answer greatly pleased Sylvester, who had no intention of going to Jerusalem and who thus thought his life was destined to be very long, if indeed he would die at all. Yet such presumption was soon shown to be mistaken, for the following year Sylvester was obliged to perform Mass on the fourth Sunday after Lent at a church in Rome named Jerusalem, whose name until then had been completely unknown to him.

And during the service, Sylvester suffered a collapse, and a few days later, on 11 May 1003, he died, thereby personally demonstrating the truth spoken by the voice issuing from the brazen head.

This prediction strangely foreshadowed that reputedly made to England's King Henry IV some years before he expired. His end came in 1413, when Henry, who was suffering from leprosy and epilepsy, resolved to make a pilgrimage to the Holy Land, but who, before he could set sail from London, was taken seriously ill. His courtiers bore him to the conveniently placed Abbot's Palace, which stands beside Westminster Abbey, where he was made as comfortable as possible in a certain chamber there, laid on a bed before the fire. But upon recovering somewhat, Henry became curious as to where he was and asked, according to the chronicler Robert Fabyan (d. 1513), 'if that chamber had any special name. Whereunto it was answered that it was named Jerusalem. Then said the King, "Laud be to the Father of Heaven! For now I know that I shall die in this chamber according to the prophecy made of me before said, that I should die in Jerusalem!" ' And indeed Henry died there on 20 March of that year, aged 47.

The above-mentioned cases are all examples of the external disembodied voice, which appears to come from a position outside the hearer. As we have seen, this point may be located close to the person's ear, or at a short distance in front of, or to one side of, or even behind him or her, or it may be situated in the air above. Alternatively, the voice can seemingly emerge from another place, such as a cupboard or from a nearby room. More rarely, the voice is heard as if at a great distance, which may, for instance, be on the other side of a river or even high up in the sky.

The second type of disembodied voice is heard internally, within the hearer's own brain, yet it is quite distinct from the voice of ordinary consciousness. For while we may not be aware of it, we all have our own inner voice, which comprises the thinking part of our mind. It cogitates in our native tongue, ruminates on our experiences and makes decisions, and is the precursor of our spoken words. It is, if you like, the 'I' within us, and we individually recognize it as being ourself. However, this 'voice of consciousness' may sometimes be interrupted by another voice, by one that is not of us, and which speaks in much the same manner as the external disembodied voice, that is, suddenly and briefly. What it says, moreover, is often revelatory, which makes it a welcome, if surprising, visitor. It occurs less frequently than its external variant, but its rarity is typically made up for by the profundity of its statements and by the inner sense of well-being and uplift that it may bring.

One person who benefited from hearing such a voice was the English journalist, essayist and author Winifred Holtby, whose last novel *South Riding*, which was published posthumously, is recognized as being a modern classic. Ill with very high blood pressure and the accompanying debilitating headaches this produced while writing the book, she was shattered to learn in due course that she was suffering from Bright's disease and might not have more than two years to live. This naturally caused her considerable mental anguish and also prompted an urgent inner need to re-evaluate her life.

Then one very cold spring morning in 1932, while staying at Monks Risborough, in Buckinghamshire, and still trying to come to terms with the fact that she might soon die, Winifred took a walk up to a farm on the side of a nearby hill. On reaching the farmyard, she noticed an ice-covered water trough nearby, beside which were standing some thirsty lambs, all plaintively bleating. Deeply touched by the sight of them, Winifred went over and broke a hole in the ice for them with a stick. As she did so, she was surprised to hear a voice speak clearly and distinctly within her, which said, 'Having nothing, yet possessing all things'. Startled by the sound of it, she automatically turned to see if someone previously unseen had spoken to her, but found that she was quite alone with the lambs. At that moment, records her friend and biographer

Vera Brittain in *Testament of Friendship* (1940), 'In a flash, the grief, the bitterness, the sense of frustration disappeared; all desire to possess power and glory for herself vanished away, and never came back ... the moment of "conversion" on the hill of Monks Risborough, she said with tears in her eyes, was the supreme spiritual experience of her life'. And happily, Winifred Holtby lived for longer than her specialist had thought possible, for she did not die until 29 September 1935, at the age of 37 and just four weeks after completing work on *South Riding*.

A similar inner voice once spoke to the headmaster and author Frederick Crossfield Happold, although the meaning of what the voice said was not immediately apparent to him. He describes the incident, which happened in early February 1913, when he was a student at Cambridge, in his book entitled *Adventure in Search of a Creed*. The hearing of the voice was preceded by a mystical experience that took place one morning when Mr Happold was alone in his room at Peterhouse. He suddenly found that the room became 'filled with a Presence, which in a strange way was both about me and within me, like light or warmth'. His awareness of this incredible 'Someone who was not myself' lasted for several hours, and it was, he comments, 'very wonderful and quite unforgettable'.

The following day, not long after the remarkable presence had finally faded away, there came the internal verbal pronouncement mentioned above, which Mr Happold regarded as 'a continuation and completion of that I have described; it "felt" the same ... This time, however, it seemed that a voice was speaking to me. It was not sensibly audible; it spoke within me. The words were strange: "Those who sought the city found the wood: and those who sought the wood found the city." Put into cold print they sound nonsensical. Yet I felt vividly that they meant something very important, that they were the key to a secret.'

It was not until many years later that Mr Happold realized that the enigmatic words spoken to him meant in essence exactly what the celebrated German mathematician and mystic Nicholas of Cusa (fl. 1430) had centuries earlier, in his book *The Vision of God*, described as 'the coincidence of opposites'. The term means in effect that all opposite qualities, forces and tendencies in the universe, like light and darkness, heat and cold, hardness and softness, good and evil, strength and weakness and so on, are only apparently dissimilar, for they are really all part of a unity, which is God; that in fact the One is many and the many are One. This concept, which is beyond human intellectual understanding and which is only comprehensible to those who have had direct knowledge of God, is at the heart of mystical experience everywhere.

Indeed, Nicholas of Cusa says of God that 'Thou, Lord, dost stand and move at the same time, at the same time Thou dost proceed and rest'. And for those who seek God, who lies both within and outside our world of apparent multiplicity, he adds that, 'Thus 'tis beyond the coincidence of opposites that Thou mayest be seen, and nowhere this side . . . for Thou art there where speech, sight, hearing, taste, touch, reason, knowledge, and understanding are the same, and where seeing is one with being seen, and hearing is with being heard, and tasting with being tasted, and touching with being touched, and speaking with hearing, and creating with speaking.'

The American psychologist Julian Jaynes, the author of *The Origin of Consciousness in the Breakdown of the Bicameral Mind* (1976) once received a similar spoken message, which however was heard externally, although unlike F.C. Happold, he never understood the meaning of what was said to him.

Dr Jaynes describes the incident in Chapter Four of his bestselling book, wherein he argues that before human consciousness developed, people everywhere were told what to do and how to behave by hallucinated voices, which were thought to be those of the gods. His experience occurred at the end of a week spent wrestling with 'the question of what knowledge is and how we can know anything at all'. Then, having fruitlessly exhausted himself with such cerebration, he lay down one afternoon to rest on his couch, when 'suddenly, out of an absolute quiet, there came a firm, distinct voice from my upper right which said, "Include the knower in the known!" It lugged me to my feet absurdly exclaiming, "Hello?" No one was there! Not even behind the wall where I sheepishly looked.'

The clarity and nearby location of the voice and the brevity of its utterance were exactly like those voices I have previously described. Dr Jaynes regarded it, however, as an hallucination, and was no doubt temporarily worried for his sanity, although it proved to be the key event in his life, leading at it did to his hypothesis about the origin of consciousness and to his celebrated book. And he adds, 'I do not take this nebulous profundity as divinely inspired.' But unfortunately, he entirely missed the import of what was said to him, although the reader, having read what Nicholas of Cusa wrote about the 'coincidence of opposites' and God, who is 'where seeing is one with being seen, and hearing is with being heard, etc.', will perhaps understand what the voice meant. The knower and the known are in fact one and the same, which is why, as the voice so clearly told Dr Jaynes, we should 'Include the knower in the known'.

The above examples of disembodied voices and what they said reveal that the phenomenon is far more complex and interesting than might at first be thought. To dismiss them as temporary hallucinations is a knee-jerk, materialistic explanation. For while most of the voices were heard by people suffering some degree of mental or emotional stress, which might seem sufficient to engender such an hallucination, many of the individuals concerned, myself included, went through far more difficult periods in our lives than the one in which the voice was heard, but without hearing another. Hence the simple equation – stress or upset equals hallucinated voice – cannot be justified. Moreover, if this causal association were true, then we would perhaps expect the person suffering from the greatest stress to generate the longest message to himself, which does not in fact happen.

However, what is perhaps most damaging to the temporary hallucination hypothesis is the fact that there are a number of cases on record, several of which are discussed later on, where two or more people have together heard the same disembodied voice and words at the same time.

But while what is said is normally brief, the message imparted shows considerable variety. Dr Johnson, for example, heard his own name called, while Graeme Moore, who had no interest in horse-racing, heard the name of a winning horse thrice repeated. Mrs West was reminded of the ring she had lost (and was assisted in finding it), while the imprisoned Benvenuto Cellini was instructed to pray to God and was later told to do as he thought best. As a young man I was seemingly advised to keep a tighter rein on my heart, while many years later my deceased wife spoke to me. The sick Mr Blackman heard a most beautiful voice speak but unfortunately missed what it said. The dying and distressed Winifred Holtby was counselled that she already possessed what is truly worthwhile. The whereabouts of his death was predicted to Pope Sylvester II. And Frederick Happold and Julian Jaynes were both given the key to understanding the nature of God, but only the former came to appreciate the knowledge he had received.

These short disembodied utterances of advice, guidance and prophecy were, in themselves, all benign and helpful. And we shall meet with many more in later chapters. Yet behind such unasked for benevolent assistance there lies a terrible irony. For one of those helped in this strange way, whose life was saved by a timely disembodied warning, went on to become one of history's most evil dictators and mass murderers.

2   The Spoken Name

Her lips were trembling and bloodless, cold drops of perspi-
ration stood upon her forehead, and in an instant after,
exclaiming in a piercing tone, 'Hark! they are calling me
again! it is – *it is the same voice;* – Oh no, no! – Oh my God!
save me, Betsy – hold me – save me!' she fell forward upon
the floor.

From *Singular Passage in the Life of the Late
Henry Harris D.D.* by Thomas Ingoldsby

It is a startling experience when a person hears his or her own
name called out by a disembodied voice, but it is none the less
something that happens quite often. Less frequently, the voice
may say the name of someone else, who may either be known
or unknown to the hearer.

I began the last chapter by mentioning that Dr Samuel
Johnson had once heard his mother call out his name in this
way. His biographer James Boswell records 'that one day at
Oxford, as he was turning the key of his chamber, he heard his
mother distinctly call - *Sam*. She was then at Lichfield; but
nothing ensued'. As Johnson was a student at Pembroke
College, Oxford from 31 October 1728 until he he left the
university without a degree in the autumn of 1731, the incident therefore took place sometime between those two dates.

The discussion by Johnson of this remarkable phenomenon
happened at a dinner party he gave for Boswell and several
other friends on Easter Sunday, 15 April 1781. Johnson in fact
brought up the subject, for after he had talked for a while about

apparitions, Boswell writes that 'he mentioned a thing as not infrequent, of which I had never heard before, – being *called*, that is, hearing one's name pronounced by the voice of a known person at a great distance, far beyond the possibility of being reached by any sound uttered by human organs.' The reason why Boswell added 'but nothing ensued' after saying that Johnson's mother was in Lichfield when the lexicographer heard her call out his name, was because Boswell himself was later told of another instance when a recognizable disembodied voice was heard, which apparently accompanied the person's death. He writes:

An acquaintance, on whose veracity I can depend, told me, that walking home one evening to Kilmarnock, he heard himself called from a wood, by the voice of a brother who had gone to America; and the next packet brought accounts of that brother's death.

This indicates that even at that time there was a widely-held belief that the hearing of a voice calling one's name meant that the person whose voice it was had just died. Yet while several of the cases mentioned below support this notion, such a voice does not always signify death, as it did not for Johnson's mother.

However, before we leave the eighteenth century, there is another case worth considering that occurred not long after Dr Johnson's experience. It was reported in a letter to *The Gentlemen's Magazine* for April 1752, which was written by the man to whom it happened, Charles Williamson, although his name is actually given as 'Charles W–m–n'. He recounts how he heard the voice of his father thrice call out to him, even though the latter was not then in the vicinity.

At the time, Charles Williamson was an apprentice draper and worked in a shop standing directly opposite the house of his father, where in fact he still resided. It was usual for him to go home and take lunch with his father each day, which he would do when his father shouted across to him that the meal was ready. At noon on Monday, 23 August 1736, when the incident took place, Charles was standing at the doorway of the shop accompanied by his employer or mistress, her maid-servant, and a gentleman named Bloxham, who delivered goods for the local drapers' supplier. Charles and his mistress were together examining a pattern or sample book and trying to decide what to order from it. Just then, he writes:

I heard my father's voice call *Charles*, very audibly, as accustomed. I answered, *Coming*, Sir. – Being intent on viewing the patterns, I stayed about four minutes, when I heard the voice a 2nd time call *Charles*. The maid heard it then as well as myself, and answered, *He is coming*, Mr Williamson. – But the pattern book not being gone through with, I was impatient to see the end, and being also unwilling to detain the gentleman, I still tarried. Then I saw the door open, heard my father call a third time in a strong, emphatical, angry tone, and shutting the door I heard its sound. – Both my mistress and the maid heard this last call; on which she pushed me out of the shop, with *Sirrah, get you gone, your father is quite angry at your stay.*

But if Charles Williamson was startled by his father's angry and impatient tone, what happened next dumbfounded him. For he hurried across the road, only to find to his surprise that the front door of the house was locked. He therefore walked around to the back gate, entered through it and passed his mother-in-law, who was in the yard, and went into the house, 'where I found no father, nor any appearance of dinner. Returning, I enquired of (my mother-in-law) for my father; she said he was not come home, nor would dine at home that day.'

So young Charles returned to the draper's shop, where he astonished his mistress and maid by relating what had occurred, and he was distressed to learn from the maid that such a thing meant that he would soon die. Indeed, he relates that 'from that hour I thought of nothing but dying, and kept myself in constant preparation for and expectation of it'.

What is particularly interesting about this case is that the absent father's voice was heard by Charles Williamson's mistress and by her maid, and presumably by Mr Bloxham. This surely discounts the possibility that the sound of the elder Mr Williamson's voice was caused by an expectation of his call, and was therefore an hallucination, particularly as all concerned were concentrating on choosing patterns at the time, and also because of the unexpectedly angry tone in which the voice spoke. Anyhow, such anticipation would have been strongest in Charles, whereas the last call was certainly heard equally clearly by the others with him. And where the associated opening and closing of the front door is concerned, and its subsequent locking, this does not necessarily mean that the older Williamson played some outlandish prank on his son, for it will be remembered that Benvenuto Cellini was once physically thrown across his cell by invisible hands.

However, despite the maid's dire and somewhat odd interpretation of the event, Charles Williamson did not die. Yet the hearing of his father's disembodied voice did have a marked and arguably beneficial effect on his character. Indeed, he adds that it immediately changed him from being 'a lad of raised spirits and extreme vivacity, which might perhaps in time, have led me into all manner of snares and pleasures of the present age', into someone who was 'fresh formed, of a grave saturnine disposition, few words, despising the present vanities and vices of the world, and associated with very few youths from that time after.'

And neither was the voice a sign, as we perhaps might more reasonably have expected, that his father had expired. But strangely, another family member did die, for Charles ends his letter by saying that, 'it is very remarkable, that I had an only uncle (who was gunner of the *Biddeford*, then stationed at *Leith*), that died there that same day, and about the same hour'.

The French astronomer Camille Flammarion (1842–1925) not only made important observations of double stars and star drift, but founded the Société Astronomique (1887) and the observatory at Juvisy (1888), as well as writing several popular books on astronomy. He also had a keen interest in psychical research, and he collected numerous accounts of ghostly happenings which seemed to suggest that there is survival after death. These he obtained through requests for such information published in various newspapers and magazines. Several correspondents described to him how either they or those known to them had heard a disembodied voice calling their name, which often turned out to belong to someone at a distance (often a loved one) who was at the point of death. A consideration of four of these cases is worthwhile in order to note the circumstances in which they occurred. This may help us to determine how they happened.

For example, on Saturday, 29 July 1865, a French student named Nephtali André was aboard a sailing vessel taking him across the Mediterranean to Algeria, where he was going for a holiday. Quite suddenly, he heard the voice of his father distinctly call out his name. Startled, he looked around immediately, but found that there was nobody nearby. Yet knowing that his father was ill and having heard 'something of the wonders of telepathy', he made a note of the time. And indeed, when he reached the port of call, he learned that his father had died 'at the same hour when he had heard [him] call "Nephtali!"'

Another instance is that of Narcisse Destrube, the musical director of the 114th Regiment, who was roused from sleep one night between midnight and one o'clock by the sound of his father's voice calling out his name. He answered him and jumped out of bed, thinking that his father had for some reason come to Saint Maixent, where he was stationed. But to his surprise Narcisse found that neither he nor anyone else was there. However, the next morning a telegram arrived bearing the unhappy news that his father, who lived many miles away at Vaubecourt, had 'died the same night and at about the same hour.' And when Narcisse went to the funeral, he was told that his name was the last word spoken by his father before he expired.

In both these cases we might be tempted to agree with Nephtali André that telepathy or thought-transference was the means by which the two fathers' voices were heard. For although we are only told that M. Destrube called out his son's name, it is probable that the elder André also did the same thing or at least was thinking about Nephtali on his deathbed. Yet if thoughts can somehow be sent across the miles from one mind to another, why should the voice heard seem to come from outside the hearer and not from within his own head? The latter manifestation, like a bad dream, would certainly be capable of waking someone asleep, which would make the production of an hallucinatory external voice quite unnecessary. And anyway, in most cases of telepathic contact, the 'contactee' reports that he thought about the person at that time or 'had a feeling' that something was wrong. This suggests that telepathy, while seemingly a plausible explanation of the disembodied voice, is not necessarily the means by which the phenomenon occurs.

The other obvious possibility is coincidence. Yet while this might be a reasonable supposition had the two sons simply thought about their fathers at the same time that each of them lay dying – for many sons often think about their father, particularly when they know he is seriously ill – coincidence is far less plausible where the hearing of a disembodied voice is concerned. After all, neither young man had heard one before, and probably did not again. Hence the odds of Narcisse Destrube hallucinating the voice of his father calling out his name at the very moment that M. Destrube actually did so must be several millions to one against. Too high in fact to be at all likely.

Yet it is a well-known fact that telepathic contact generally happens between people who are emotionally close to one another, which doubtlessly explains why laboratory experiments testing the phenomenon never produce results that are convincingly above chance. Moreover, where family members, close friends and lovers are concerned, telepathic contact between them typically takes place during a crisis, which naturally generates more intense thoughts in the victim than would occur in normal circumstances.

But while this emotional link suggests that telepathy was possibly the means by which the two young men heard their fathers' voices, it does not explain why those standing with Charles Williamson in the shop doorway, who had no close emotional ties with his father, also heard the elder Mr Williamson's voice call out.

In fact the hearing of a disembodied voice by several people who had no close emotional tie with the person to whom the voice belonged, is a feature of another nineteenth-century case recorded by Camille Flammarion. This happened in Switzerland (the exact date is uncertain), and it was reported to Flammarion by John Junot, one of the family group who heard the voice, some years afterwards.

John Junot said that one night, when his parents, four sisters and himself were in bed asleep, they were all suddenly awakened by a loud voice calling out their father's Christian name, Florian. The voice then repeated the name, but less loudly, and finally once more, when it was little more than a whisper. His father recognized the voice as that of a friend of his named Renaud, who lived in Paris, and being startled by it and not knowing from where it had come, he went to the front door to look outside, fully expecting to find that Renaud had somehow made his way to their home. But there was no one there, and neither were there any footprints in the fresh snow to indicate that he or anyone else had come to the door.

The answer to why Renaud's disembodied voice was heard came a few days later, when Florian Junot received a letter from Paris informing him that his friend had been run over by a bus and fatally injured. It also related that Renaud, as he lay dying in the street, had called out 'Florian!' several times. And while John Junot does not actually say that Renaud's death took place at the same time that his voice was heard, the association of the two events is implied.

In this case we have seven sleeping people who were

together woken up by the disembodied voice of Florian Junot's friend Renaud, and all of them heard it twice more. Yet only Florian knew Renaud well, and it was he that Renaud was thinking about and called out to as he died. This fact in itself suggests that telepathy was not the cause of his voice being heard by all the Junot family, for if it had been then surely only Florian would have heard him speak.

It might of course be argued that even though the other family members had no close emotional tie with the man who died, they did at least know him quite well, which might in itself be sufficient to allow telepathic contact. However, later on in the book I shall describe cases where several, and on occasions many, people have together heard an unknown disembodied voice at the same time. It is difficult to explain such unexpected anonymous verbal contacts by telepathy.

But to demonstrate that the situation is by no means clear, I shall describe one more case collected by Flammarion. The dramatic events took place in the early hours of Monday, 18 March 1907 and they centred around a young married woman named Jeanne D., who was asleep alone in bed, her husband being away on business. Suddenly, at about two o'clock in the morning, she was woken by the sound of her name being called three times. The voice, Jeanne noticed, came from the corridor outside her bedroom. Startled, she sat up, thinking that her husband must have returned home for some reason. Yet when she went and looked out into the corridor, she found to her astonishment that no one was there. Now somewhat frightened, she woke up her maid, who slept in the next room, and together they made a search of the house, but discovered nothing amiss. Both women then went back to bed.

Jeanne eventually fell asleep again, but she was soon awakened by her name being twice called out, the voice now sounding as if it came from someone in great distress. Alarmed, she jumped out of bed and shouted to her maid that she must surely have heard it too. But the maid, who was still awake, replied that she had heard nothing. Then both women went nervously around the house again, but failed to find anyone there. So they reluctantly returned to bed.

But that was not the end of the matter. Half an hour later, while lying awake in a state of trepidation, Jeanne heard her name called out for the last time, the voice sounding even more distressed than before. Hardly surprisingly, she did not go to sleep again that night.

A few days later Jeanne at last learned why she had heard the voice. The reason was tragic in the extreme, and yet it was not without a strange beauty. A relative of hers, paying a visit from Noyon, where her former fiancé lived, disclosed that on the night in question the man had died of tuberculosis, which had been preceded by a 'most violent dyspnoea' or laboured breathing, during which he had called out her name several times, while yet lying in his wife's arms.

This case likewise suggests that there was a causal link between the dying man in Noyon crying out 'Jeanne!' several times and the repeated hearing of her name called by his former fiancée, the first somehow bringing about the second, rather than the two events being merely coincidental. But none the less, it is odd that the maid, lying in bed in the next room, did not hear the second two calls or for that matter the third, when she was awake at the time. After all, she certainly heard Jeanne D. when she shouted out to ask her on the second occasion if she had heard the voice as well.

Yet before we jump to the conclusion that this means the voice was an hallucination prompted by telepathy, we should remember that we do not know, nor can we know at this late date, the volume of the disembodied voice or how loudly Jeanne had to shout to make herself heard by the maid. For it may be that Jeanne's shout was much louder, and that the quieter disembodied voice, particularly if it sounded from outside Jeanne's bedroom door, was simply not audible to the maid.

Indeed, the following British case certainly suggests that disembodied voices are not produced by telepathy. The incident took place at Edinburgh on 12 November 1960, although it was not made public until 1999, when it appeared in the July issue of the *Paranormal Review*, published by the Society for Psychical Research.

At 10.30 a.m. on the Saturday in question, writer Marion Law was sitting at her kitchen table typing an article, when she suddenly heard a voice say 'Mum – Mum' in her right ear. The words, moreover, were immediately followed by a loud noise resembling, she says, 'a bundle of chains being dropped from a height on to a concrete floor', which made her jump to her feet. Then came a bang like 'the bathroom door being slammed loudly'. And even more bizarrely, these startling sounds were accompanied by 'a sensation of a strong wind blowing through the hall just outside the kitchen door'.

Mrs Law quite naturally assumed that both the call and the noises must have been made by her 14-year-old son Angus, and she hurried into his bedroom to tell him off. Yet to her astonishment she found that Angus was fast asleep in bed. Even more confused, she sat on the other bed, which belonged to her eldest son Iain, who was then abroad serving with the RAF in Singapore, where she suddenly 'had the strangest feeling that (he) was there'.

But none the less, she woke Angus up and asked him about the call and the noises, and he, with a puzzled yawn, denied having made them, since he had been slumbering in the arms of Somnus.

That afternoon a telegram arrived bringing the sad news that Iain had been seriously injured in a motorcycle accident, from which he in fact died the next day. The time of the accident was given as 5.30 p.m., but because local Singapore time is seven hours ahead of Greenwich, it was 10.30 a.m. in Glasgow. 'This meant,' remarks Mrs Law, 'that I had actually heard my son's voice in his last few seconds of consciousness, followed by all that noise of the crash.'

But although it might still be argued that Iain's voice was conveyed by telepathy to Mrs Law, it presumably cannot account for the accompanying sounds of the crash, and if they could manifest 'out of thin air' some 5,000 miles away, then there is perhaps no reason why his voice could not do the same.

And indeed, an unusual sound alone can sometimes signal a person's death. One of the most curious in this regard is the howling of a banshee, which traditionally happens prior to the demise of certain members of the aristocracy, although strange knocks or raps, as if made by ghostly knuckles on a door or window, are more common. The sound of ethereal music has also been reported, like that heard in the case mentioned below, and the drum beaten by the so-called Tedworth drummer has passed into folklore. Other cases where ghostly music has been heard are considered in a later chapter.

Lastly, where death and a calling voice are concerned, I must relate a beautiful Canadian Indian example, which is generally regarded as a legend, but which, if we read it with the above cases in mind, is almost certainly true.

It is said that one evening before the coming of the white man a young Cree brave was paddling his canoe down a river in what is now the province of Alberta, heading towards the village where his beloved lived, in order to ask for her hand in marriage. Suddenly, he heard his name called from the darkness underneath the trees at the river's edge. The voice seemed familiar to him, and it sent a shiver down his spine.

He cried out fearfully, 'Who calls?', but at first he heard only the sound of the wind in the trees and the rippling of the water. However, shortly afterwards he heard the voice again, this time calling his name clearly as if from the air nearby. Now he had no trouble in recognizing it as the voice of his beloved, although it seemed to belong to a spirit rather than to a living woman.

Shocked, and scarcely believing what he heard, the brave woefully enquired 'Who calls?' again. But there was no answering response, and he was left with only the familiar sounds of nature. So he continued his journey, paddling throughout the night with an increasingly heavy heart, and he arrived at his destination early the next morning. On bringing his canoe to the shore, he noticed a group of women gathered around the tepee of his dearest love, who were singing the traditional songs of death. He knew immediately that his sweetheart had died.

On asking when this had happened, the young brave was told that it had taken place the evening before – and that before she died she had twice called out his name. He murmured that he had heard her spirit call to him, and tearfully related how he had called out to her. Then brokenhearted, he returned to his canoe, paddled away from the village, and was reputedly never seen again. Yet his story so touched the villagers, that in his memory they renamed the river *Katapaywie sepe*, which means 'Who calls?' Today it is better known by its French equivalent, the Qu' Appelle River.

These cases all support the old belief that hearing a known disembodied voice calling out your name is a sign of that person's death, yet as I have indicated above, this is not always true, for such a call may equally be prompted by a non-fatal accident or other crisis. The four following examples of the latter type were collected by the American psychical researcher Louisa Rhine. None is dated, but they probably all happened in the 1950s.

The first, which is reported by Mrs Rhine in her book entitled *Hidden Channels of the Mind*, happened to a North Dakota woman, who was in her living room one evening, when suddenly she heard her son's voice clearly call out 'Mom!' behind her. But the boy was not there, being two-hundred miles away at boarding school. The woman later learned that on that evening, and at the same time she heard his voice, her son had broken his arm in a basketball game, which had caused him a great deal of pain and distress.

In *The Invisible Picture* Mrs Rhine describes the similar experience of an Ohio mother. She was washing up dinner dishes one summer evening when out of the blue she heard her son Stan's voice call out 'Mom!' three times. His voice came, or so it seemed, from outside the kitchen door. But young Stan was then five miles away attending a picnic. Quite naturally, the woman felt that Stan had maybe been hurt in some way, but without knowing how. However, not long afterwards she received a telephone call from one of the picnic organizers, who told her that Stan had been accidentally knocked unconscious whilst playing baseball, but that he had none the less fully recovered. Indeed, the boy suffered no lasting damage from the blow he had received.

Although Mrs Rhine does not say that the first boy called out 'Mom!' when he broke his arm, we may reasonably assume that he did. Yet a direct link between the moment of injury and the hearing of Stan's voice is lacking in the second case, as Stan was knocked unconscious. But it is possible that he called out to his mother when he came to, or that he at least thought about her then.

But the hearing of a known disembodied voice by someone at a distance does not only occur in crisis situations. Such an event can also happen when the person concerned has simply been called out to by the owner of the voice, either by mistake or because he or she is feeling lonely.

Louisa Rhine, for example, quotes the case of the young woman in Los Angeles, who one night heard the voice of her absent mother call out her name from the next room. She automatically answered her, but then realized that her mother, who lived on the other side of the country, was not there. The apparent cause of the disembodied voice was revealed a few days later, when the girl received a letter from her mother, who wrote that on that night, 'I was so lonesome for you that I stood in the doorway of your room and called to you.'

Equally interesting is the experience of the young man who went to work at a department store in Wisconsin, situated about 400 miles away from his family home and his mother. One day, while serving a customer, he heard his mother's voice call out his name from behind him, and he automatically turned and replied, 'Yes, mother?' He was naturally surprised and somewhat embarrassed to discover that she was not there, and could only explain to the customer that he had thought he had heard his mother speak to him.

When he told his mother about the incident in a letter, she replied by saying that at the time she had been working in the garden and had wanted a hoe, which had made her, without thinking, look towards the house and shout out to him 'fully expecting an answer'. She then had realized that he was not there and had 'felt funny' about calling to him.

Less often, the disembodied voice which calls out a name may be that of someone who is dead, or alternatively the voice may be completely unknown to the hearer, who thus does not know if the person to whom it belongs is living or not.

Mary Rose Barrington, an Honorary Spontaneous Cases officer of the Society for Psychical Research, recently told me how in 1972 her mother Minerva Barrington was startled one evening to hear the disembodied voice of her late husband call out to her. Mrs Barrington was sitting up in bed reading at the time, when she suddenly heard his voice cry 'Min!' from the next room, which had formerly been his bedroom, much as he had done when he was alive.

This occurrence is unlikely to have been an hallucination caused by wish-fulfilment or by expectation, because Mrs Barrington did not believe in survival after death and because her mind was fully occupied with her book. Moreover, her husband had died ten years earlier, in 1962. This naturally suggests that Mr Barrington's voice was somehow able to manifest in the vacant bedroom, from where it was heard by his widow. But why should it have done? The reason may lie with Mrs Barrington's recent return to the house after an absence of several years. Indeed, her daughter remarks, 'I suppose one might speculate that if my father really had anything to do with it he was signifying that he knew she was back in her old room'. But she adds, 'I have to say that it was not so "old" as all that, because they had lived here for less than a year when he died'.

But sometimes, as the following example shows, there is a clear reason why the voice of a deceased loved one is heard to speak. And the length of time between the two events can be correspondingly much shorter.

When Edward Wratten of Dorsetshire died in 1985, his wife Dorothy was devastated by his loss. The couple had enjoyed a happy marriage, although Edward, a large, robust man, had never been backward in chiding her when he thought she was being too emotional or 'silly' for any reason. His call from the next realm happened a week after his death, when Dorothy had one evening gone tearfully to bed, only to begin crying, as she told me, in a desperate, destructive manner.

Then suddenly, to her complete astonishment, she heard Edward's voice say – 'Dorothy!' – loudly and clearly, speaking in the same tone that he had used in life when he was reprimanding her. Indeed, he had formerly only used her Christian name when he was annoyed with her and wanted her attention, preferring at other times to address her as 'darling' or with some other form of endearment. His disembodied voice came, Dorothy said, from her right, seemingly from a specific area about 6 feet away, close by the bedroom door, and between 5 or 6 feet above the ground. It was followed by a resonance or vibration of the air, and the two events shocked her into hiding herself under the duvet, where she lay for about half an hour before falling asleep. She then slept soundly throughout the night, waking the next morning feeling refreshed and comforted. And while she did weep for Edward on other occasions, she never mourned him so heart-rendingly again. His voice had told her, in other words, to pull herself together, and it perhaps also spoke to let her know that, while he had physically died, he still existed, albeit in a form invisible to the eyes of the living.

Sometimes the reason for the called name may lie in a prior agreement made between two or more people, to the effect that whoever dies first will try to get in contact with the other(s) in some way afterwards. These 'post-mortem' pacts are quite often made by married couples and by close friends. Not all are successful, but one man who did hear his wife's voice after her death was a London resident named Nigel B., a member of the Society for Psychical Research, who told me that he and his wife had 'discussed many times the question of communicating with the other one as soon as it was possible in the post-mortem state'. They had, in other words, made such a pact.

Nigel's wife died from a heart condition in February 1992. Her death in fact followed a long illness, but while Nigel was thus somewhat prepared for her passing, he found that his 'grieving was more than I could have imagined'. None the less, there was no immediate post–mortem communication from her, and indeed as the weeks and months went by Nigel gradually forgot all about their pact.

But then one night towards the end of September, seven months after she had died, his wife kept her promise. Nigel went to bed at about 10.30 that evening, sitting up reading for a while, with his back and head against the upturned pillow, the bedside lamp on to provide the necessary illumination. It was not long, however, before he unintentionally dozed off. This is what happened next:

I was woken up by my wife's voice calling my name in my *left ear only*, although both my ears were clear of the pillow. Her voice was a very strong, clear whisper: *'Ni-gee'*. It was quite unmistakable. This was my wife's nickname for me over 30 years ago. It was a greeting she used to use when meeting me to give me some good news and when she was very happy. This was no dream. There was no ambient noise in the bedroom. My neighbours were away.

Again, I think we can fairly say that Nigel's dead wife's voice was not caused by expectation or wish-fulfilment, for Nigel was not necessarily expecting to hear her speak (they had only agreed to try to communicate, which can be done in a number of ways), and he had by then forgotten about their agreement. And that night, he had gone to sleep reading a book, so that his mind was previously occupied with its contents. This suggests that it really was his wife's voice that woke him, which had somehow been able to articulate close to his left ear.

Such post-mortem voices may sometimes be more frequent and persistent. The famous Italian astronomer Galileo Galilei (1564–1642), for example, often heard his beloved eldest daughter Maria Celeste's voice calling to him after she died from dysentery in April 1634.

Occasionally an *unknown* disembodied voice is heard calling out a person's name. An example of this strange manifestation took place in the spring of 1994, when such a voice unexpectedly called out the name of one of the three employees working at The Star inn, located at Norman's Bay, East Sussex, not long after closing time. And like the ominous meaning of the spoken names mentioned earlier, the voice was an apparent harbinger of death. My informant was Dan Slatter, one of the three people present, who described the occurrence in the following way:

It was after the pub had closed and we had finished clearing away and washing-up glasses, etc. There was myself, the manager John and another member of staff still on the premises and it must have been a little after midnight. We sat down at a table to have a quiet drink. The only lights were those behind the bar. Then we heard a soft male voice just say 'John'. We all looked at each other and the other member of staff went to look in the kitchen/restaurant area, as this was where he thought the voice came from. I went to look in the games room area as this was where I thought the voice came from, and John went to check the toilets and cellar in case someone had been locked in. None of us could find anyone, so we all sat down again and commented how strange this was.

Thus the voice, as far as they could reasonably ascertain, had no genesis in the human world, and was therefore an anonymous disembodied voice. It was also unusual in having no clearly identifiable point of origin. But the reason for its sudden speaking of John's name became clear not long afterwards, for Dan adds: 'I don't know if this is significant, but a few weeks later John [the manager] suddenly got backache and it was diagnosed as spinal cancer. Sadly, he died a few

months later.' The fact that the three men concerned, none of
whom was expecting such a vocal pronouncement, together
heard the voice indicates that it had an external point of
origin, that is was not, in other words, a trick of the mind or
an hallucination, perhaps produced by telepathy, for surely
only John would have heard his name called if that had been
the case. Hence the call may have originated from a dead
person (perhaps a relative) who was at that moment able to
verbally 'get through' to John and who was heard by the
others at the same time – or it may have been spoken by his
'guardian angel' or by a similar spiritual entity. Such entities
are considered in a later chapter.

Another unknown voice that spoke equally mysteriously
was heard by a young man named Les Wood in the same year,
although it thankfully was not a forewarning of his death.

Les, a resident of Liverpool, told me that when he returned
home from work one day, he went up to his bedroom and lay
down on his bed to take a short rest. Then about five minutes
later, much to his surprise, he suddenly heard a young female
voice clearly say 'Leslie' in his left ear, the sound seemingly
coming from about six inches away, as if the person concerned
had leaned over and spoken to him. But none the less, there
was no one there.

The voice, Les said, spoke his name softly and affection-
ately. He also commented that it was unusual for him to be
addressed as Leslie, because everyone knew him as Les. He
got up right away to see if he could find out who it was, but
there was nobody in the house apart from his parents, who
were downstairs watching television. Neither had called out
to him. To this day he does not know why the intriguing voice
uttered his full Christian name, or indeed why it did so. He
had never heard a disembodied voice before, and he has not
heard one since.

3 The Advisory Voice

One night the hermit had a dream, and heard a voice from
heaven, which commanded him to say to his companion that
he must without delay go to the Holy Land, and fight against
the heathen.

From *Legends of Charlemagne* by Thomas Bullfinch

In the first chapter I mentioned four examples of disembodied voices that offered unexpected and direct advice to those
who heard them. Thus I was counselled by a disembodied
voice not to lose my heart too easily; Benvenuto Cellini was
told on one occasion to pray to God and on another to do
what he thought was right; and Julian Jaynes was instructed to
'Include the knower with the known'. These helpful disembodied utterances happened during moments of distress, and
were surprising not only for their unexpectedness but for the
aptness of their advice, even though Julian Jaynes failed to
appreciate what was said to him.

The advisory disembodied voice is in fact perhaps the most
frequently heard and useful *longer* manifestation of this
remarkable phenomenon. It manages to say in a sentence or
two exactly what should be done by the hearer, and if the
advice is followed, it invariably produces a beneficial result.
Sometimes, however, what is said is comforting rather than
strictly advisory, whereas on other occasions the voice utters
an instruction which, while advisory in a general sense, saves
the person who hears it from serious injury or death. Such
warnings are considered in the next chapter.

But while most people do take the advice given to them by

a disembodied voice, some are more cautious, as was a friend of the writer, folklorist and psychic researcher Andrew Lang (1844–1912).

In *Dreams and Ghosts*, Lang describes how the man concerned, when a boy, was uncertain about which of two career paths he should take. This led to him to pray earnestly to God for guidance, and shortly afterwards he 'heard an *internal* voice advising a certain course'. When Lang asked him if he had heeded the advice offered, his friend replied, 'No, I didn't. I considered that in my circumstances it did not demand attention'. His reaction is both strange and unusual, if not somewhat arrogant, because he had asked for divine help, but refused to take it when given.

The following early example of a disembodied advisory voice is one of the most remarkable on record. Not only did the voice give succour to the man to whom it was addressed but it was also heard by many other people. The latter fact suggests that it was a genuine external phenomenon, and was not therefore given to those who heard it by telepathy and then exteriorized as a mass hallucination.

The occurrence took place in AD 155 at Smyrna (modern Izmir), a seaport on the Ionian coast of what is now Turkey, which was then a part of the Roman empire. At that early date Christianity was in the process of attracting converts and establishing itself as a major religion, which had caused growing anger and hostility towards Christians among the pagan majority. Indeed, they not only regarded Christianity as a foreign superstition, but they accused Christians of atheism and claimed they were evil participants in 'Thyestean feasts and Oedipodean intercourse', or in other words, of eating their own children and fornicating with their mothers!

That year, during the week-long festival dedicated to Titus Antoninus, the Emperor, a group of such Christians, who had previously refused to pay homage to him, was thrown into Smyrna's amphitheatre, in order to provide entertainment for the populace by fighting with wild beasts. Yet when they refused to defend themselves against the lions and other carnivores, the pagan spectators angrily demanded that their bishop, Polycarp, be brought to the arena and made to suffer the same demand and, if necessary, the same punishment.

The Roman proconsul, wishing to please the crowd, therefore ordered that a search be made for Polycarp, and the elderly bishop was eventually found and arrested by soldiers at a farmhouse some way outside Smyrna, where he had taken refuge. But when Polycarp, on being brought into the city, refused to recognize the divinity of Caesar, the arresting sheriff had no choice but to order him into the amphitheatre. And remarkably, according to a letter afterwards written about Polycarp's martyrdom by the church at Smyrna to the church of Philomelium, this is what happened next:

As he was entering the stadium, there came to Polycarp a voice from heaven, 'Be strong, Polycarp, and play the man'. And no one saw the speaker, but the voice was heard by those of our people who were there. Thereupon he was led forth, and great was the uproar of them that heard that Polycarp had been seized. Accordingly, he was led before the Proconsul. . . .

But the Proconsul, not wishing to harm the 86-year-old man, simply asked him to 'Swear by the genius of Caesar'. This Polycarp also declined to do, whereupon the Proconsul said, 'Swear, and I will release thee; curse the Christ'. But again Polycarp refused, which caused the now-angry Proconsul to ask him a third time to swear by the genius of Caesar. When this appeal was also rejected, the Proconsul told Polycarp that if he did not change his mind, he would have him thrown to the wild animals. Polycarp, however, replied that he would rather face death than deny his God, which so enraged the Proconsul that he instead ordered the bishop to be burned alive. The order was quickly carried out, although the burning was also accompanied by a miracle, for the church of Smyrna's letter continues:

We, to whom it was given to see, beheld a marvel . . . The fire took the shape of a vault, like a ship's sail bellying in the wind, and it made a wall round the martyr's body; and there was the body in the midst, like a loaf being baked or like gold or silver being tried in the furnace. So at length the lawless ones, seeing that his body could not be consumed by the fire, bade the executioner approach him to drive in a dagger.

When the Proconsul demanded of Polycarp that he should swear by the *genius* of Caesar, he was not talking about the Emperor's intellectual ability but rather about the guardian spirit (or tutelary deity), known to the Romans as a genius, that was believed to guide him in his imperial deliberations. In fact the ancients thought that we all have such a guardian spirit, which not only acts as a counsellor and advisor but also watches over us throughout our lives. Today we call its restraining influence our conscience. Certain early philosophers even taught that we have two such accompanying spirits, one good and the other evil, that vied with each other for our attention, the first trying to make us behave well, the second trying to tempt us into behaving badly. Similar spirits, known as *genii loci*, were also believed to inhabit specific places.

This idea, while seemingly heathen in concept, finds a parallel in the guardian angels of Christian belief, one of which is likewise said to accompany each of us throughout life. But whether the spirit is called a genius or a guardian angel, it does form a possible source of those anonymous disembodied voices which are heard from time to time, such as the one mentioned above that advised Polycarp to remain true to his faith. Indeed, the fact that Polycarp did not think he had been spoken to by God suggests that this may well be true. I shall say more about such vocal guardian spirits when I discuss the tutelary spirit or, to use the Greek term, *daimonion* of Socrates later on.

An advisory disembodied voice may also have been heard by St Augustine, the author of the famous *Concerning the City of God against the Pagans*, just over two hundred years later. The saint tells us in his *Confessions* that he had lived a debauched youth and was then very undecided about Christianity, despite the fact that his mother was a devout convert to the faith. However, one summer's day in AD 386, when Augustine was in a state of inner turmoil, being torn between the temptations of the world and the Christian promise of deliverance from sin, he went into the garden of his mother's house and sat tearfully under a fig tree. There he suddenly heard a childlike voice call out repeatedly from a nearby garden, '*Tolle, lege; tolle, lege* . . .' or 'Take it, read it; take it, read it . . .'

Augustine had never heard the chant before, which persuaded him that it was not an ordinary child's voice, but rather one that came from heaven. He therefore took up the copy of St Paul's *Epistle to the Romans* that lay beside him, opened it, and studied the first passage on which his eyes fell. He was astonished to find that it read: 'Let us walk honestly, as in the day; not in rioting and drunkenness, not in chambering and wantonness, not in strife and envying. But put ye on the Lord Jesus Christ; and make not provision for the flesh, to *fulfil* the lusts *thereof*.' (XIII, 13–14)

Augustine had no need to read on, for he tells us, 'as I came to the end of the sentence, it was as though the light of confidence flooded my heart and all the darkness of doubt was dispelled'. He was, in other words, immediately converted to Christianity, and he became in due course one of the most influential of the early church fathers.

More oddly, however, two voices may sometimes be heard, whose respective advice is contradictory, which seems to support the ancient idea that each of us has two spirit guides or *genii*, one of which is good, the other evil. A famous case of such dual counselling took place in the thirteenth century. Its subject was an attractive young woman named Margaret, a native of the Tuscan town of Laviano. She was unfortunate in having a bad start in life, for her mother died when she was seven years old, and she was cruelly treated thereafter by her peasant father's second wife. However, on reaching young womanhood, and seeking escape from her unhappy home, she became the mistress of a nobleman at nearby Montepulciano, with whom she lived for the next nine years and to whom she bore a son. Such a domestic arrangement, however, was considered shocking and wicked at the time.

Yet in 1273, while out one day visiting his estates, the nobleman was attacked, murdered and mutilated by a gang of robbers. Tradition says that Margaret was apprised of his death by his small pet dog, which ran back to his castle and, by barking and whining, induced her to follow him. The dog led her to the body of its master, and Margaret, shocked by the dreadful sight, believed the murder was a judgement by God on her sinful way of life. And wishing to turn over a new leaf, she went with her young son to her father and begged him to forgive her, but he, at the urging of her stepmother, refused to have anything to do with her.

Stumbling tearfully away from his door, Margaret made her way into a nearby vineyard, where she sat down and tried to decide what to do next. It was then that a disembodied voice – which she afterwards described as belonging to a 'demon' – spoke to her and advised her to carry on as before, saying she would soon find another lover. But not liking this advice, Margaret prayed earnestly to God, begging Him for guidance, which soon came in the form of an inner voice that said, 'Margaret, go to the Franciscan convent at Cortona and humbly ask for admission'. This she hastily did, but the friars, knowing of her loose reputation, were at first reluctant to consider her application, but they changed their minds when she demonstrated the sincerity of her repentance. After undergoing a three-year period of probation, during which she and her son were the guests of two ladies, Marinana and Raneria, who had taken pity on them, she was admitted into the Third Order of St Francis, and thereafter lived a most holy and increasingly secluded life, converting many by her prayers and by her good counsel. She died in 1297, and was canonized in 1728, becoming known as St Margaret of Cortona.

An advisory voice was heard on request by Dr Richard Napier (1559–1634), who was rector at Great Linford, a village in north Buckinghamshire, from 1590 until his death, and who, upon gaining a license to practise medicine in 1604, became well known for his healing skills. Moreover, in his youth he had studied astrology, then an essential medical accessory, in London with Simon Forman and at which he apparently excelled.

But Dr Napier's curative abilities did not stem from either his medical or his astrological knowledge, but rather came from the helpful advice he received from a disembodied voice, which he believed was that of the angel Raphael. When a patient came to consult him, Dr Napier went into his closet to pray for guidance, whereupon the voice would tell him whether or not the patient was curable, and if he or she was, it would impart a remedy.

John Aubrey, in his *Brief Lives*, mentions one example of the angelic voice at work. In 1625, Sir Francis Wyld brought his eight-year-old grandson, who was suffering from worms, to Dr Napier for treatment. The doctor retired as usual to his closet, where he fell on his knees in prayer, and was duly given a prognosis by the voice. The child, it revealed, would recover from his infection at age 14 (which he apparently did), and it added that he would gain relief by drinking a small quantity of sweet Muscat wine every morning. The remedy was slow but none the less effective in the long term.

Hence the voice of Raphael, in addition to being advisory, was also predictive, and I shall mention one or two other of its predictions in the chapter devoted to such disembodied pronouncements.

Yet it is more common for an advisory voice to speak directly to the person concerned about health matters. Two odd nineteenth-century examples are worth repeating in this regard. The first, quoted by William James in *The Varieties of Religious Experience*, is from the biography of Billy Bray, who 'had been a smoker as well as a drunkard' and who began hearing 'a small, still voice within speaking to me'. Thereafter every time Billy took up his pipe to smoke, the voice said: 'It is an idol, a lust; worship the Lord with clean lips'. And at last Billy, on being asked by a woman friend if he did not think it was wrong to smoke, threw his tobacco into the fire and crushed his pipe under his foot, and never smoked again.

Similarly, in *The Psychology of Religion*, Edwin Diller Starbuck quotes the case of a 53-year-old woman who had unsuccessfully tried to stop smoking and who had prayed repeatedly to God for help in overcoming the habit. Then one day, while she was sitting by the fire smoking her pipe, she said that 'a voice came to me. I did not hear it with my ears, but more as a dream or sort of double think. It said: "Louisa, lay down smoking." At once I replied, "Will you take the desire away?" But it only kept saying: "Louisa, lay down smoking". Then I got up, laid my pipe on the mantel-shelf, and never smoked again or had any desire to. The desire was gone as though I had never known it or touched tobacco.'

A recent and far more dramatic example of direct medical assistance given by a disembodied voice was reported in an article appearing in the 20–27 December 1997 issue of the *British Medical Journal.* Its Nigerian-born author, Dr Ikechukwu Obialo Azuonye, a consultant psychiatrist at the Adult Mental Health Unit of Lambeth Healthcare NHS Trust, described how early in 1984 he had been consulted by a middle-aged, married European woman (whom he identifies as A.B.) worried about an inner voice she had begun hearing. This had introduced itself one evening while she was reading, by saying, 'Please don't be afraid. I know it must be shocking for you to hear me speaking like this, but this is the easiest way I could think of. My friend and I used to work at the Children's Hospital, Great Ormond Street, and we would like to help you.' Not long afterwards the voices, in order to demonstrate their sincerity, 'gave her three pieces of information, which she did not possess at the time. She checked them out, and they were true.' But none the less, A.B. began to suspect that she was going mad and therefore sought help from Dr Azuonye. Because she had had no previous mental problems, he treated her with medication (thioridazine) and counselling, and when the voices stopped speaking to her, he believed that she had been cured.

But not long afterwards, while still taking thioridazine and having gone on holiday abroad, the two voices began addressing her again. They warned A.B. that there was something seriously wrong with her and urged her to return immediately to England for help. When she arrived back, the voices gave her an address to go to, which remarkably turned out to be the computerized tomography department of a major London hospital. 'As she arrived there, the voices told her to go in and ask to have a brain scan for two reasons – she had a tumour in her brain and her brain stem was inflamed.' And astonishingly, when the brain scan and other tests were carried out, with the support and recommendation of Dr Azuonye, the voices were shown to be entirely right. Indeed, the tumour was a meningioma the size of a large hen's egg and needed urgent attention.

A.B. was therefore quickly admitted to the hospital and emergency surgery was carried out, which undoubtedly saved her life. And when she came around from the anaesthetic, the voices spoke to her one last time, saying 'We are pleased to have helped you. Goodbye.' She has not heard from them since. This remarkable case led Dr Azuonye, who has been practising psychiatry for 17 years, to observe:

This is the first and only instance I have come across in which hallucinatory voices sought to reassure the patient of their genuine interest in her welfare, offered her a specific diagnosis (there were no clinical signs that would have alerted anyone to the tumour), directed her to the type of hospital best equipped to deal with her problem, expressed pleasure that she had at last received the treatment they desired for her, bid her farewell, and thereafter disappeared.

Taken together, these startling occurrences suggest that the voices were not hallucinatory, as Dr Azuonye claims, but had somehow actually come from the people whom they said they were. And while the voices did not say if 'they' were alive or dead, we can perhaps surmise from their description of themselves as having once worked at the Children's Hospital in Great Ormond Street, that they were deceased doctors formerly employed at that establishment.

These unknown disembodied voices were unusual in that they spoke on several occasions and because they also gave the woman concerned specific instructions, notably the address of where she should go to receive the medical help she needed.

Another case in which an unknown disembodied voice spoke in the guise of a guardian was recently recounted to me by the woman who had the remarkable experience. It likewise suggests that there are invisible entities or *genii* that have a protective function in our lives.

Jean Akerman, a resident of Porthcawl, in South Wales, said that in 1956, when she was only 19 years old, she contracted a serious lung disease. The treatment included a long, difficult operation to remove the infected area, which required Jean to come all the way to Brompton Hospital in London to have it carried out. She was naturally very frightened about the operation, not least because she was alone and far from her home and family.

. The day before it was due to take place, Jean went into the church beside the hospital, where she sat down in a pew, bowed her head, and prayed to God for His help. Then suddenly, she sensed there was someone standing behind her, and in the next moment she heard a man's voice, speaking in a strong, clear tone in her left ear, say to her, 'Jean, don't worry, you're going to be all right. I'm going to take care of you.' And as the voice spoke, she felt a hand placed comfortingly on her left shoulder. Startled, she turned to see who it was, but to her complete astonishment she found that there was no one there. So she hastily stood up and looked around the church, but saw that although there were one or two others praying as she had been, no one was near enough who could possibly have been responsible for either the voice or the touching hand.

'It was just uncanny,' Jean said, 'but I felt completely at peace as I left the church. All my fear had gone, and the operation was a complete success. Indeed, I'm still here today!'

Equally astonishing in this regard is the case of a London man named Mike, who received timely assistance when gambling, and who, when he tried to continue on his own, learned an important lesson about the financial hazards of such an activity.

Mike told me that one night he went into a casino to play blackjack, at which he lost steadily. But when he was down to his last two £1 chips, he suddenly heard a male voice from behind him say, 'Go and play on the centre box at the next table.' Mike spun around to see who had spoken to him, but found to his surprise that there was no one there. Yet while dumbfounded by this, he took the voice's advice and moved to the table indicated, where he resumed playing the card game. And thereafter, whenever he was dealt a new hand, the helpful voice advised him whether to bet or not. This disembodied assistance continued until Mike had won back the £123 with which he had begun playing. At that moment, the voice said, 'OK, you're on your own now.'

But instead of quitting while he was ahead, Mike bet unaided on the next hand he was dealt and lost the lot. He then left the casino with no money in his pocket, but instead with the directly imparted knowledge that gambling is a mug's game and that he should waste no more time and money on it. And he has not gambled since!

Two English lorry drivers have also related to me their experience of hearing a disembodied voice, the first of whom once heard the voice of his deceased mother, the second that of an unknown person or entity which has spoken to him on several occasions, often to warn him about hold-ups on the road ahead.

When the mother of trucker Yorkie died, he was as upset as any son would be, especially as she had passed away after a somewhat protracted illness, which left him wondering how she was faring in the next world. Then one morning a week after her death, while he was performing his ablutions in the bathroom at home, he suddenly heard, to his complete amazement, his mother's voice, speaking externally and clearly, say to him, 'I'm all right now'. And despite at first wondering if he was going off his head, Yorkie found consolation in her words, which reassured him that she was happy and contented where she was.

Lorry driver Jeff Bayliss first heard a disembodied voice a few years ago when he was driving down to Felixstowe docks. There was a hold-up on the road ahead and Jeff was about to take a particular side road to try to avoid it, but suddenly, before he could turn off, a voice speaking within him warned, 'Don't go this way!' He was understandably startled by the unexpected pronouncement, but he none the less took the advice offered, selected another route, and reached his destination without too much delay. And Jeff says that the same male voice has given him similar warnings on other occasions. In this respect he was helped rather in the manner of Socrates by his guardian spirit or daimonion. Then early in 1999, which was the last time the voice spoke to him and when he was again on the road, it said, 'Ring your mother'. He therefore called home immediately, and learned to his dismay that his mother had been taken ill. He accordingly cut short his trip, and returned home to help look after her.

A moving example of an advisory voice is recounted by Louis E. LaGrand in his article entitled 'Extraordinary Experiences of the Bereaved' which appeared in the November 1996 issue of *The Psi Researcher*. Mr LaGrand writes: 'I remember a young woman telling me of hearing the voice of her father after she arrived home from his funeral. She had gone upstairs to her room for a brief respite and as she closed the door she felt a hand on her shoulder and her father say, "Take care of your mother." His voice was as clear and convincing, she said, as though he was standing right next to her.'

The incident had the same property of unexpectedness which characterizes any disembodied voice, while at the same time providing comfort to the young woman, who was thereby informed of her father's continued existence in the next realm of being. Indeed, her father evidently not only still knew what was happening to her, but he was sufficiently concerned about his wife's well-being to be able to 'get through' to her vocally. And the experience, like that of Jean Akerman, was heightened by the accompanying touch of his hand on her shoulder.

Another comforting advisory voice spoke to a young American infantry soldier during the Second World War. According to Dr Raymond Moody in *Reflections on Life after Life*, one day when the GI's platoon was advancing through a village, enemy aircraft were suddenly sighted and he and some of his comrades hurriedly took cover in a burned-out building, although their position was observed by one of the Luftwaffe fighter pilots. As the German dived his plane towards them and began firing, the shells first struck the ground, making a visible dust path towards the ruined house. Their approach badly frightened the watching soldier, who felt sure that they were all going to be killed. But just then, he reported, 'I felt a wonderful comforting presence there with me, and a kind, gentle voice said, "I'm here with you, Reid. Your time has not come yet!" I was so relaxed and comfortable in that presence.' And indeed, as the anonymous disembodied and possibly divine voice had promised, the GI survived the aerial attack unscathed.

In her book *Things I Can't Explain*, Margaret Gordon Moore relates how the disembodied voice of her late husband gave her some vital financial advice. This happened not long after her solicitor, who had been appointed by her husband as the trustee of her financial affairs, told her one evening that the price of the American shares in which the bulk of her fortune was invested had dropped sharply, and he advised her to sell them before they went any lower. Mrs Moore was both shocked and upset by this, not simply because the shares had lost about £40,000 in value but because the solicitor should have apprised her much sooner of the market downturn. When the man had gone, she went into her sitting-room and tried desperately to decide what she should do.

I was very young, apprehensive, and alone, and began to consider selling the remainder of the stock. [Then] in the quietude of the little room, a voice clear and distinct said firmly: 'Don't sell this stock. If they have lost £40,000 there are only five to lose. Risk this yourself; it cannot go any lower, it must rise. Do not sell.'

My astonishment was sincere, but even to me at that amazing moment, this seemed excellent sense and good reasoning. I felt a load taken off my mind, and slept well that night.

On the following morning, when her broker telephoned to ask for permission to sell the shares for her, Mrs Moore, to his complete surprise, told him not to sell them. She also asked him to keep her informed of their price each morning for the following couple of weeks. This he did, and soon gave her the news that the price had begun rising again. When he asked her if he should then sell them, the voice again told Mrs Moore, 'Don't sell.' This continued for some little while, until the voice gave her further advice, instructing her 'to sell half of the sum realized and invest in gilt-edged security, leaving the other half where it was'. She again did as it suggested, her confidence coming from the fact that 'I did know it was my husband's voice, and I followed his advice faithfully and fearlessly to the great advantage of my future welfare and the children's.'

The unknown disembodied voice which spoke in 1991 to Jean Woodbridge, of Barnstaple, Devon, likewise gave her some much-needed advice and comforted her. Jean's beloved son David died in April of that year and she was overwhelmed with grief by his loss. Unfortunately, the tragedy also had an adverse effect on her marriage, which was already in some difficulty, and Jean and her husband began having frequent arguments and shouting matches.

Then one night about six months after David's death, following another row with her husband, Jean went upstairs to bed feeling totally drained and defeated. She sat miserably for a while on the end of her bed, blaming herself for the upset and wondering how she could sort things out, and then began getting undressed. Suddenly, without it in any way being expected or hoped for, a clear disembodied male voice spoke to her, which 'came in my right ear (and) seemed to go right through my head. It said: "Be gentle with yourselves, you do not have the experience to cope in this situation." '

As might be expected, Jean Woodbridge was completely flabbergasted by the sudden pronouncement and could not understand where the voice had come from. But she none the less felt uplifted by the wonder of hearing it, and that night she slept better than she had for long time. The advisory words gradually brought home to her the fact that she was selfishly concentrating on her own grief and pain while ignoring her husband's anguish, and that she should stop being so hard on him and on herself. This realization helped her to reach out to him.

I slowly became less engrossed with my own feelings and grief, and much more open to the pain of others and the way that they expressed that pain, including my husband . . . I did become more gentle, more aware of other people's feelings, and less wrapped in my own pain. Without that change in me the marriage would not be continuing as it is now.

The voice that Jean heard therefore had a profound and positive effect on her by helping her deal with what had become an almost impossible situation. And while she and her husband did separate for a while in order to give themselves space to come to terms with everything, they 'stayed very much in contact' and are now happily back together again.

Another woman who was counselled by a disembodied voice is cited by Louisa Rhine in *Hidden Channels of the Mind*. Yet in this case, the voice was known to the hearer and it originated from a female friend, who lived over one thousand miles away.

The woman who heard the voice was a New Jersey resident named Marion, who had been brought to the end of her tether by family worries, poor health, and sleeplessness. Then one night in 1947, feeling that life was no longer worth living, she began to think of ways in which she might kill herself. 'When suddenly,' she reported, 'as clearly as if she were in the room, I heard the voice of a dear friend say: "Don't do that, Marion!".'

The sound of the voice and its message jolted Marion out of her self-destructive frame of mind, and she thought no more about committing suicide. Yet because her friend, an older woman who had become like a second mother to her, lived in faraway Florida, Marion assumed that her own disturbed, over-tired mind must have somehow created the illusion of hearing her voice. But such a notion was dispelled the following day, when a special delivery letter arrived from her friend. It revealed that she had been suddenly woken in the middle of the night by an overwhelming feeling that all was not right with Marion. She had therefore got out of bed and had spent the rest of the night praying for her.

'Her letter was proof to me,' said Marion, 'that somehow she had been aroused from her sleep by my great need and she had reached me over all those miles to comfort and protect me. It was one of the most beautiful and mysterious experiences I had ever had.'

The case is made doubly remarkable by the prescience of the woman in Florida, who had somehow sensed the anguish of her young friend, perhaps by either clairvoyance or telepathy, and by the fact that she was thereafter able to 'send' a spoken advisory message to her. But because we are not told if she actually said the words 'Don't do that, Marion!', we do not know if they were a direct manifestation of what she said or if they were rather a verbal summation of her fears and prayers.

The next case, which is included in *Apparitions*, written by

Celia Green and Charles McCreery, is worth considering because of the difficulty in determining whether or not the voice heard was hallucinatory.

In 1954 a young woman volunteer was sent to Immingham, in Lincolnshire, to help repair a sea wall that had been damaged in the bad floods of that year. She spent her first day there being shown the full extent of the damage, but when night fell and work stopped, she and her guide had an evening meal, after which he suggested that they went to see a film at the cinema in Grimsby. She was happy to do this, and they fortunately found seats for themselves in the circle of the otherwise full cinema. But then something entirely unexpected happened.

The lights were dimmed and everybody stopped talking, settling back in their seats for the start of the performance. Then a voice said to me loudly and distinctly, 'You can't do it, you know.' It was so clear and resonant that I turned and looked at my companion who was gazing placidly at the screen, then I looked at the people round about but nobody evinced the slightest interest in anything but the film being shown. I was amazed and somewhat relieved when it became apparent that I was the only person who had heard anything.

The woman thereafter began to doubt that she had actually heard a voice, and she was still doubting its reality when it spoke to her again two weeks later. She was then in bed, just about to drop off to sleep, when the same 'loud, clear and compelling' voice spoke exactly the same words to her, although this time she was sure that if anyone had been in the room with her, they would not have heard anything. And she goes on to add: 'At the same time I was confirmed in a belief which had grown since the first time I heard the voice, and that was that some subconscious part of myself was advising me that I could not do the job I had undertaken.'

The voice was certainly advisory, but was it, as the woman evidently believed, an hallucination or was it disembodied? It certainly seemed to come from outside herself, and yet if it had, then why didn't anybody else in the cinema hear it? But none the less, it is relevant to point out that the woman only started to think that she wasn't up to the job when the voice first told her that it was too much for her. Hence in this regard it was seemingly a catalyst. Thus her doubts about her abilities began with the voice, and were confirmed, as she says, by it later repeating the same message.

However, it could be argued that when she was being shown the amount of work required of her she subconsciously apprehended that she was not up to the task, but did not allow herself to think it. The voice therefore became the way in which she permitted herself to do that. Yet there is no evidence for this. Not only had she volunteered for the job and was keen to help, but our minds do not ordinarily function in such a circuitous manner. After all, she consciously viewed the flood damage and was shown what was required of her, which would surely have allowed doubts about her capabilities to be considered at the same time. She may not have liked expressing them, but they certainly were not of such momentous psychological importance that they would have been immediately suppressed. And besides, her mind would only have been delaying the inevitable if it had behaved in such a roundabout way.

This suggests that the voice was a genuine disembodied one, which offered her advice, rather than being an hallucination. But if so, then why wasn't it heard by the other people at the cinema on that first evening? This is more difficult to answer, but two possibilities do present themselves; firstly, the voice may have spoken directly to her brain's hearing centres, which somehow prompted the illusion that it came from outside herself; or secondly, that whatever said the words from an external point was able to alter subtly the nature of the sound waves created, so that they were only perceptible to her.

The voice that advised 25-year-old artist and illustrator Adam Graff to end the happy relationship he was in is quite different from most of those that I have thus far considered.

For a start, the voice was an internal one which spoke to him on numerous occasions during a three-month period. It also began in a less certain way, appearing at first more like a thought than a definite voice. Moreover, because Adam eventually took the voice's increasingly insistent advice, he has no way of knowing whether it counselled him wisely or not. And like many people who have heard a voice, he was also reluctant to talk about it for a long time, 'fearing that my sanity would be questioned'.

The voice tentatively began in the summer of 1994, shortly after Adam and his girlfriend of three years, whom he had however known all his life, came back to England from their first holiday together in the Sinai. He told me:

We returned home. I moved out of my parents' house and rented a room in Walthamstow. Our relationship remained consistently loving, but soon I heard my first message, simply that I must end the relationship. . . . The voice gave me the same message again sometime later and I thought it to be just a thought of my own and not a voice, even though I was not ready to end the relationship. I ignored the 'thought/voice' and continued to enjoy my relationship.

However, while Adam tried to get on with his life, the voice would not go away. He found this both worrying and upsetting, not least because he had always been very happy with his girlfriend and with their time spent together. But as the weeks went by the voice became more clear-cut and persistent:

The message continued more frequently and with more force, and I could identify it as not my own thought but a voice from outside of me, a male voice who had a message to pass on to me. I told it that I was not ready to end the relationship, and not to bother me. This pattern continued over maybe three months or so. The message was never any more than 'You must end the relationship', but increasingly pressing until it became so frequent and eventually

65

with such force, almost aggressive, that I felt weak and had to comply.

Adam in fact took the voice's unasked for advice and broke up with his girlfriend, telling her, as the voice commanded, that it had to end. Hardly surprisingly, she was both hurt and shocked by this, while he felt that he was 'being forced to do something that I didn't want to do'. And what made matters worse was Adam's inability to explain to his girlfriend exactly why he was breaking up with her. However, once the deed was done the voice stopped and has never spoken to Adam again. He and his ex-girlfriend have fortunately managed to remain good friends, while she afterwards met and married someone else.

This is an unusual case, but we can perhaps assume that the voice advised Adam to end his seemingly happy relationship because there was something wrong with it that he was not aware of consciously, and which would have brought him great unhappiness or even tragedy had it continued. And while the voice appears to have arisen from his own thoughts and to have evolved out of them, this may merely be an expression of its difficulty in getting through to him. For the communicating intelligence, which may have been Adam's own guardian spirit, having recognized a real danger to him in the relationship, was required to interact directly with the physical world, which cannot have been easy for it. Indeed, as we have seen, most disembodied voices can only manage to impart one word or a single sentence, whereas the voice that spoke to Adam was able to repeat the same message, rather like a Morse SOS tapped out by a telegraphist with a head wound, intermittent and barely comprehensible at first but gaining force and clarity as the injured party returns fully to his senses.

Another case happened in March 1726. But despite its early date and the fact that the voice was only advisory in a general sense, it is nevertheless of great interest, not simply because two people in separate rooms clearly heard the disembodied voice of a loved one who was some distance from them, but because the latter dreamed she was present with them at the time.

Writing in *The Gentleman's Magazine*, correspondent John Walker describes how one evening in the above month, a young Bristol woman named Molly, who was ill with small-pox and who was being cared for by her mother, unfortunately died from the infection. Her mother was alone with her, owing to the fact that her husband, a clergyman, was then staying at his church residence over 20 miles away, accompanied by their other daughter. But not long after Molly expired:

her Sister, who was at her Father's, being in bed, heard the Voice of her Mother lamenting herself upon the Death of her Daughter. This much surprized her knowing that her Mother was then as far as Bristol. When she arose in the Morning, her Father, seeing her look much concerned, asked her what was the matter with her? Nothing, says she: Her Father reply'd, I am sure something is amiss, and I must know what it is. Why then, Father, says she, I believe my Sister Molly is dead; for this night I heard the voice of my Mother lamenting her Death: says the Father, I heard the same myself, and her Voice seemed to me to be in my Study.

The father and daughter received confirmation of Molly's death the next morning when a letter came bearing the sad news. And two or three days later, the body of Molly was brought to the church for burial, accompanied by her mother, who was then able to tell them about the events of that unfortunate night. And what she revealed was astonishing, for she said that as soon as Molly had died, she felt so exhausted by weariness and anxiety, that she lay down on her bed and fell fast asleep, whereupon she 'dream'd that she was with them telling her Grief for the Loss of her Daughter. This surprized them; and asking the Time, it appeared to be much the same in which they heard her Voice.'

As I briefly mentioned in Chapter One when considering the case of Mrs West, the living human body contains a replica of itself, known as the double, which can on occasions leave the body and appear at a distant place. When this happens the consciousness may go with it, so that the person is aware of being at that place. Since such a conscious double separation occurs most commonly when someone is asleep, the scene or events seen by it are often considered to have been a dream when the double returns to the person's body and he or she awakes.

Such a conscious double separation appears to have taken place when Molly's mother fell asleep, and her double was then translocated some 20 miles away to the abode of her husband and other daughter, where she loudly expressed her grief at Molly's loss, which she had not been able to articulate until then. Her double evidently manifested in her husband's study, from where her groans and cries were heard, as John Walker's letter reports, by both her husband and daughter, thereby apprising them of Molly's death. And when her double returned to her body and she awoke, she recalled her presence in the study as being a dream.

The double is a replica of the entire body and it is seemingly quasi-physical in nature, for it can not only manipulate objects, but when the consciousness separates with it, it can also speak, an act which requires the expulsion of air from its chest over its duplicate vocal chords. And while it usually reflects light and thus becomes visible to others, it can perplexingly sometimes remain invisible, so that its voice, when heard, seemingly emerges from thin air. This fact may well explain the phenomenon of the external disembodied voice in many cases, and similarly, because the double retains its integrity after death, when it is known as a wraith, it may likewise be responsible for many post-mortem contacts.

Finally, it is relevant here to consider what is perhaps the most famous case of a disembodied advisory voice, which was heard by four people at the same time. The incident is described in the New Testament books of *Matthew*, *Mark* and *Luke*, and happened when Jesus took three of his disciples, Peter and the brothers John and James, with him to the top of a high mountain. Shortly after they arrived Jesus underwent what is known as a transfiguration, whereby his face became as bright as the sun and his clothes a brilliant white. Two other figures next appeared beside him, whom the disciples recognized as Moses and Elijah, who spoke with Jesus. As they talked a shining cloud appeared over them all, in whose shadow they stood. Then from the cloud a disembodied voice said, 'This is my dearly beloved son, with whom I am well pleased – listen to him.' This so terrified the disciples that they threw themselves face down on the ground and did not move until Jesus went to them and touched them reassuringly, and said, 'Get up and don't be afraid.' And when they rose to their feet they saw that Jesus was then alone and that the cloud had gone. He told them to say nothing about what they had seen until after his death and resurrection.

The voice that spoke was apparently that of God Himself, although unfortunately no description is given of what it actually sounded like, which accords with many of the other accounts of such voices. Yet the accompanying transfiguration of Jesus and the ancient Biblical figures seen with him suggest that it was. And although these features of the experience are unique in themselves, they too find parallels in the touching hands that are sometimes felt when a voice is heard. But more importantly, because the voice came from out of the air and said the same short, one-sentence advisory message that we have seen characterizes such pronouncements, we can be assured by this that the event happened as described and that Jesus Christ was indeed the Son of God.

4 The Warning Voice

Vale went forth to seek silent-footed Hodur. Through the wood of blackness he went, for he had knowledge of where the blind god was hidden. Then he heard a voice which cried: 'The avenger cometh, O slayer of Balder.'
From *Teutonic Myth and Legend* by Donald A. Mackenzie

As I mentioned in the last chapter, the warning voice is a variant of the advisory voice, for it tells a person either to do or not to do something in order to save him or her from some upset or disaster. The warning may require an immediate response, or it may apprise the hearer of an event that is soon going to happen. The latter implies a foreknowledge of the future and in this regard the warning voice is therefore sometimes a prophetic voice, although I shall deal with those which are unequivocally prophetic in the next chapter.

Aside from the disembodied voices mentioned in the Bible, the most famous ancient example is the voice which regularly addressed the Greek philosopher Socrates (469–399 BC). This he believed came from his *daimonion* (pronounced 'themoneeon') or accompanying tutelary deity or spirit. At that time, everyone was thought to have such a spirit guide, which entered the world with them at birth and which remained with them throughout their lives. It is the equivalent, as I have earlier noted, of what Christians today call a guardian angel.

However, the Greek word δαιμονιον (daimonion), when latinized and shortened, becomes daemon or demon, and because Socrates was a pagan and thus, in this regard, a supposed soft touch for the Devil, his demon was interpreted by early Christians as an evil spirit, which is why the word acquired the devilish associations that we are familiar with today. This is unfair and unfortunate because the daimonion of Socrates only ever gave him good and moral guidance, which is hardly something that a Christian demon would do.

It is to be regretted that Socrates, like Jesus Christ, did not write anything down, because all we know about his life and philosophy comes second-hand from the works of others, the two most important being Plato and Xenophon, his former pupils. Yet they both mention his daimonion, and Plato, writing in his *Apology*, which purports to be the speeches made by Socrates at his trial for allegedly corrupting the youth of Athens, represents him as saying, 'It began in my early childhood – a sort of voice which comes to me; and when it comes it always dissuades me from what I was proposing to do, and never urges me on.' In fact it was Socrates' claim that he was frequently counselled by a divine voice that formed part of the charges made against him: he was accused of inventing new gods and of not acknowledging the old ones.

The evidence we have indicates that the disembodied voice heard by Socrates was an internal one, that it regularly spoke to him, often interrupting him in the middle of a sentence, and that it thereby made an important contribution to his philosophic reasoning. Yet quite how it counselled him is uncertain because Plato and Xenophon, the two main authorities on his life, say seemingly contradictory things about it. Plato, as we have noted, represents Socrates as saying, 'It always dissuades me from what I was proposing to do, and never urges me on', whereas Xenophon maintains that 'This voice gave him notice of what he should do'. But they may in fact be saying essentially the same thing, for if the voice told Socrates what he should not do, then it was *ipso facto* telling him what he should do.

Xenophon further reveals that Socrates' daimonion often also prompted him to warn his friends against pursuing a particular course of action if it would have an unfortunate outcome, and that 'they who believed him, and followed his advice, always found advantage by it; as on the contrary, they who neglected his admonitions, never failed to repent their incredulity'.

For example, Socrates once warned his friend Crito not to take the country walk he was about to set off on, but Crito paid no heed to him and went anyway. But on the walk, while attempting to pass through some undergrowth, Crito pushed aside the branch of a tree, which on being released, flicked back and struck him painfully in the eye. When Socrates later met the wounded and bandaged Crito, he was not surprised to hear about his accident, and said: 'Naturally; for having received my usual divine admonition, I attempted, unsuccessfully, to dissuade you from going on that walk.' This in turn suggests that the voice did not tell Socrates what was going to happen to his friend, but only that he should not go for a walk that day.

Two other examples of a more momentous nature are worth repeating here. In 424 BC Athens went to war with neighbouring Boeotia, and suffered a serious defeat in the battle fought near the town of Delium. The Athenian army, which included both Socrates and Xenophon, was obliged to flee from the battlefield, and most ran to and followed the main road back to Athens. Yet Socrates, arriving at its start somewhat later, accompanied by the Athenian general Laches and by Alcibiades, told them that his daimonion had warned him not to take the same road, and they accordingly followed a longer and more circuitous track. And it was fortunate that they did, for the Boeotian cavalry went in pursuit of the Athenians, caught up with those retreating along the main road, and slaughtered many of them and took the rest prisoner, whereas Socrates and his companions successfully evaded them and eventually returned safely to Athens.

Similarly, two Athenian citizens named Timarchus and Polemon once plotted secretly together to murder an enemy of theirs. On that evening Timarchus, in order to provide a cover for his planned activities, invited Socrates and some other friends to his house for dinner. When the prearranged time came for meeting Polemon and committing the murder, Timarchus told his guests that he was slipping out for a while but would not be long. Socrates, however, by listening to his voice, warned him that it would be best for him not to leave the house. Surprised by this, Timarchus sat down again, although a little later he once more rose to leave, whereas Socrates told him a second time to stay where he was. Again Timarchus sat down, yet becoming agitated by the passage of time, he waited until Socrates was talking to another diner, and then hurriedly left the room unobserved by him. He met with Polemon and together they killed their intended victim, but were unfortunately caught before they could escape. Both were tried for the crime and sentenced to death, and Timarchus, remembering the warning he had ignored, said loudly to his brother as he was led to the place of execution, that 'I die for not believing Socrates'.

Such accompanying spirits sometimes also express their guidance by touch rather than by voice, or occasionally, as happened in the cases of Benvenuto Cellini and Mrs West, by the use of both. One daimonion that only used touch is mentioned by the French writer J. Bodin Augevin in his *De la Demonomanie des Sorciers*, published in 1587 and quoted by Alexander Briere de Boismont in *On Hallucinations*. He reports that 'I have heard of a person now living who had a spirit which always waited on him, and whom he had known for more than thirty years.' This invisible being woke the man up early every morning by knocking on his door, and in addition to this useful service it gave him moral guidance and also apprised him of the intentions of others. It did this in the following way:

The spirit always accompanied him, and gave him a sensible sign, such as *touching him on his right ear*, if he did anything that was wrong, and on his *left ear*, if he did what was right. If anyone came for the purpose of deceiving him, or to take him off his guard, then he suddenly perceived the signal on his right ear; but if he was an honest man, and intended him good, he perceived the signal on his left ear . . . If any evil thought entered into his mind, and he dwelt upon it, he soon felt the signal to desist.

Hence the spirit behaved in much the same way as Socrates' daimonion, by working for the man's good. It is to be regretted that such benign invisible assistance is not more commonly experienced!

In the previous chapter I mentioned that the Greek daimonion was called a *genius* by the Romans, who also believed that they inhabited various outdoor places, when they were called *genii loci*. One such 'spirit of the place' is recorded by both Plutarch and Livy as having given a spoken warning to a Roman plebeian named Marcus Ceditius (or Caedicius), when he was walking along Rome's New Road one night in early July 390 BC. On reaching a certain spot on the road, he suddenly heard a loud disembodied voice say, 'Go, Marcus Ceditius, and early in the morning tell the magistrates that the Gauls are coming'.

Next day the startled Ceditius did as he was instructed, but the magistrates took no notice of what he told them. However, not long afterwards, as the voice had forewarned, the barbarian Gauls, led by Brennus, arrived at Rome and sacked it, with the exception of the Capitol, which was built on the city's highest and most inaccessible point. The Gauls held Rome for seven months, until at last the besieged senators on the Capitol managed to get word to their commander Camillus, whom they had previously exiled, and persuaded him, by giving him dictatorial powers, to come to their rescue. Camillus thereupon marched his army to Rome, where he found that the barbarian invaders were now starving and stricken with disease, which enabled him quickly to defeat them and send them fleeing back to Gaul.

To celebrate his triumph and his return to Rome, Camillus set about repairing the desecrated temples and erecting new ones, which included one built on the very site where the voice had spoken to Marcus Ceditius. The latter was done, says Livy, 'to expiate the guilt of ignoring the mysterious Voice which had been heard in the night prophesying disaster before the war'. It was dedicated to the God of Utterance.

Yet while we can appreciate the need of the Romans to atone for the guilt they felt by building a temple to the genius in question, we cannot help but wonder why, if the genius knew that the Gauls were coming, it did not also know that none of the magistrates would believe Marcus Ceditius when he told them what it had said. For if it did, then speaking to Ceditius was entirely pointless. The genius should obviously have spoken directly to one or other of the magistrates, who would then perhaps have heeded its warning. However, if it was a genuine *genius loci* then it may not have been able to move far from its spot beside the New Road and was thus forced to impart its warning to whoever came along first, who unfortunately happened to be a plebeian.

A much later but still ancient example of an anonymous warning voice was that heard by Samson of Tottington (AD 1135–1212), the tenth abbot of the monastery of Bury St Edmunds, Suffolk, during his first year of office in 1182. According to the *Chronicle* of Jocelin of Brakelond, Samson took a tour of the monastery's manor lands shortly after his investiture 'and from all and sundry he demanded an aid and recognition, according to the custom of the realm'. This excursion eventually brought him and his companions to Warkton in Northamptonshire, where they lodged for the night in a house. But while they were all asleep, the abbot was suddenly woken by a disembodied voice, which said urgently, 'Samson, arise up quickly,' and then 'Rise, thou tarriest too long.' Somewhat groggily, Samson struggled to his feet, wondering what on earth was the matter, but he soon discovered that one of the monks had mistakenly left a candle burning, which was about to topple over into the straw. Had the straw caught fire Samson and everyone else would have been burned alive, for there was no exit from the house, whose windows had been barred against intruders and its door locked with a key. Hence the mysterious voice, by rousing

Samson and thereby alerting him to the danger, saved all concerned from a fiery death.

Such a warning, however, is not always so readily heeded. In the following nineteenth-century case, the internally heard disembodied voice had to repeat its message many times before the man concerned took notice of what it said, although its dogged persistence eventually did prevent both him and his children from dying in a disastrous fire. This naturally suggests that the intelligence behind the voice, which may have been that of the man's own daimonion, knew of the tragedy fated to happen on that evening.

On Tuesday, 5 December 1876, while on leave in New York, an American army officer named Captain A.B. MacGowan made arrangements to take his two young sons to the Brooklyn Theatre the following night to see a performance of *The Two Orphans**, which had been attracting large and enthusiastic audiences.

'But on the day of the proposed visit,' Captain MacGowan afterwards related to Sir William Barrett, FRS, one of the founder members of the Society for Psychical Research, 'it seemed to me as if a voice within me – it was like a voice talking inside me – was constantly saying, "Do not go to the theatre. Take the boys home, take the boys home." I could not keep these words out of my mind; they grew stronger and stronger and at noon I told my friends and the

---

* *The Two Orphans* was one of the most popular melodramas of the nineteenth century. Written by Eugene Corman and Adolph Phillipe d'Ennery, it was first performed at Paris in January 1874. It soon moved to London, following which an adaptation by Hart Jackson opened at New York in December 1874. After running for 180 performances, *The Two Orphans* was taken on a four year long American tour by actress Kate Claxton, who played the part of Louise, the blind orphan, and who eventually acquired the rights to the play. Captain MacGowan would have seen Miss Claxton in the role of Louise if he had taken his sons to the Brooklyn Theatre on that fateful night.

boys that we would not go to the theatre.' His sudden change of mind upset his sons and led to his friends chiding him for being cruel and unfair to them. And indeed Captain MacGowan, feeling pressured by their disapproval and who anyway did not want to disappoint his offspring, came close to changing his mind again and so taking them to the theatre after all.

But all afternoon the words kept repeating themselves and impressing themselves upon me. That evening, less than an hour before the doors opened, I insisted on the boys going to New York with me and spending the night at a hotel convenient to the railroad, by which we could start in the early morning. I felt ashamed of the feeling that impelled me to act thus, but there seemed no escape from it. That night the theatre was destroyed by fire with a loss of some three hundred lives.

The fire in fact broke out at about 11 o'clock on the stage of the Brooklyn Theatre. Panic ensued as the flames swiftly took hold. There were about 800 people in the audience, most of whom were seated in the galleries. The fire spread rapidly through the building, causing the said galleries to collapse, thereby killing hundreds and blocking the aisles and the exits. However, most of the people on the floor and on the stage escaped with their lives, although two actors were killed. Altogether a total of 326 people were burned to death, many of whom were so badly charred as to be unrecognizable. Indeed, the Brooklyn Theatre fire of 6 December 1876 remains one of the worse disasters of its kind to have happened in the United States.

It might of course be objected that the voice Captain MacGowan heard was his own intuition or prescience, which thereby saved both him and his two sons from certain death. This is the view taken by Renée Hayes, who writes in *The Seeing Eye, The Seeing I* that 'where unnamed voices are concerned there is no problem. They are the vehicle of the impression and no more; sometimes the hearer does not even mention whether they are male or female'.

Renée Hayes goes on to relate the experience undergone by a young mother after her daughter had gone out to play at a seemingly safe place on some rocks by a sea wall. The incident in question happened at Trinity, near Edinburgh, in July 1860. The mother, Mrs W., the wife of a vicar, said that she 'distinctly heard a voice, as it were within me, say "Send for her back or something dreadful will happen to her".' Like Captain MacGowan, Mrs W. initially tried to ignore the voice, but when it spoke the same words insistently twice more, she at last sent out her maid to bring the child home. And it was fortunate that she did, as not long afterwards 'a train was derailed on the railway line running alongside the sea wall, which crashed through the wall and careered over the rocks where the girl had been playing.

Yet most people who have precognitive warnings or presentiments, which are ostensibly produced by their own ESP, invariably report that they had a 'feeling' or a sense that something untoward was going to happen, which is sufficiently strong to cause them to change what they were going to do. They do not, in other words, hear a voice. And while some cannot say if the voice they heard was male or female, there are many, as we have discovered, who report that it was distinctly male or female and who can often, moreover, identify it as belonging to someone known to them.

It is pertinent to note that, with the exception of Marcus Ceditius, none of those mentioned above was unequivocally told what disaster lay in store for either them and/or for their children or friends – although Mrs W. was warned that 'something dreadful' would happen to her daughter if she was not brought home. However, some warnings can be very specific. One early twentieth-century example of a disembodied voice that clearly informed the hearer of what would happen to him if he did what he was intending to do was recorded by Canadian folklorist Helen Creighton.

The experience happened to a Liverpool, Nova Scotia, sea captain named Godfrey. He was lying in his bunk one day prior to his vessel's departure, when suddenly a bundle of papers was thrown across the cabin at him. Captain Godfrey thought that one of his shipmates was 'having some fun', but when he looked across the cabin, he was startled to see what appeared to be a 'blaze of fire' burning in the centre of the room. Then a disembodied voice said to him, 'Don't go in this ship or you'll be lost. If you don't go you'll live to be an old man and you'll die at home.' Hardly surprisingly, Captain Godfrey left the ship the next day, but without telling anyone why he was disembarking. The vessel sailed as soon as a new captain had been found, but as the voice had predicted, it was never heard of again. Captain Godfrey, however, continued his life afloat and sailed safely all over the world, until at last he died at home in bed when he was an old man.

A called name alone can also serve as an adequate warning. An example of this is given in *The Invisible Picture* by Louisa Rhine. She describes how a young couple's lives were saved by a disembodied voice shouting out the woman's somewhat unusual name of Mina as they walked along a city street. The cry brought the pair to an abrupt halt, and as they turned to see who had called out, a large cement block fell on the pavement at the spot where they would have been had they continued walking. The voice therefore prevented them from being crushed to death. Nobody was seen either before or after the block fell who was known to Mina or her husband and who might have been responsible for the shout, which indicates that it was an authentic disembodied warning.

In her biography of her husband Peter, who became chaplain to the United States Senate, Catherine Marshall records how, when he was a young man in his native Scotland, his life was saved by a warning voice calling out his name. The experience was indeed so remarkable, that Peter, believing God had preserved him for a reason, decided to enter the ministry and thereby to devote his life to serving others.

The incident happened in the summer of 1925, when Peter

Marshall took a job in England at Bamburgh, a small town on the coast of Northumberland, made famous as the birthplace of Grace Darling (1815–1842), the lighthouse keeper's daughter who saved the shipwrecked crew of the *Forfarshire*. There is moorland to the west of the town, which is made hazardous in some places by the presence of abandoned limestone quarries.

One night when Peter was returning home on foot from a visit to an inland village, he somewhat foolishly left the road in order to take a shortcut over the moor back to Bamburgh. He knew that there was a deep limestone quarry lying close to the Glororum road, but he thought that he would easily miss it, despite the gloomy darkness of the night. But in this he was quite wrong, and unbeknownst to himself he headed straight towards the quarry and to a possible fatal fall over one of its steep sides. As he tramped ever closer, Christine Marshall writes that 'Suddenly he heard someone call, "Peter! ..." There was great urgency in the voice.' Peter stopped and responded, asking who it was and what it was they wanted, but could see no one in the darkness. When no reply came to his query, he shrugged and began walking on again. But before he had gone five paces the voice shouted his name again, more loudly and urgently than before. He stopped abruptly and stared uncomprehendingly around into the dark night, and then, moving his foot, he stumbled and fell to his knees.

Putting out his hand to catch himself he found nothing there. As he cautiously investigated, feeling around in a semicircle, he found himself to be on the very brink of an abandoned quarry. Just one step more would have sent him plummeting into space to certain death. . . . This incident made an unforgettable impression on Peter. There was never any doubt in his mind about the source of that Voice. He felt that God must have some great purpose for his life to have intervened so specifically.

But although we might agree that Peter was saved for a higher purpose, it is likely that the cry did not originate from God, but rather from Peter's own daimonion, his spiritual guardian, whose job it was to protect and preserve him.

A more recent case which involved both a called name and the apparent opening of a door happened in Halifax, West Yorkshire, on Thursday, 12 March 1970. At about 11.45 that evening, 18-year-old Margaret Bradley and her mother, also named Margaret (whom I shall refer to as Mrs Bradley for clarity), were sitting in the living room of their home drinking a cup of tea before going to bed. They were both feeling relieved by the news, obtained from a telephone call to the local hospital at 10 p.m., that Margaret's father was recovering well after the operation on his stomach ulcer he had had that afternoon, and that he was asleep.

But suddenly, to their surprise, both women heard their back door open noisily and a woman's voice shout with some urgency from their kitchen, 'Margaret, Margaret!'. They looked at one another in alarm, and Margaret cried out, 'Who could that be at this time of night?' Puzzled, Mrs Bradley replied by saying she was sure that she had locked the back door. Margaret told me:

It really frightened us, and we weren't sure which Margaret the voice was referring to, although my mother was always called Maggie. I ran to the lounge door and put my weight against it and said to my Mom, 'What shall we do?' We stood in fear some 10 minutes before a knock came on the front door. I told my mother to look out of the window and see who it was. She did this, and said with some relief that it was my brother, who was 15 years old at the time.

On being asked to check the back door, the boy reported that it was locked and said that there was nobody outside anyway. 'Our back door has a very distinctive sound as it has a metal frame and it made a noise as it opened outwards,' added Margaret. 'We knew that the door had made the sound of someone coming into the kitchen and calling out.' When her brother returned, the two women told him about the strange voice, but without being able to offer any explanation for it, particularly as neither had recognized it. Feeling uneasy about it but not knowing what it could mean, they all went to bed, but were soon roused by a loud knock on the front door. The visitor turned out to be a policeman, who brought news that the hospital wanted them to go straight there because Mr Bradley had begun haemorrhaging and it was feared that he might die. Margaret and her mother later learned that the haemorrhaging started at the same time that the calling voice was heard.

We stayed all night at the hospital and they did manage to save him on that occasion, but the following six weeks was a very anxious time because my father suffered one setback after another. He eventually was told that he could come home and asked my Mom to take his clothes on to the hospital but Mom felt uneasy whilst packing them. This proved to be right as we received a telephone call saying that my Dad was having to go back into the theatre for a second operation from which he died on the 1st May 1970.

On that first night, Margaret's married eldest sister also received an intimation that all might not be well with their father, although this was entirely different from the called voice. Margaret explained: 'She said that earlier that evening when she had gone to bed she woke up and saw my father's face in her bedroom and he was smiling at her. She said it was so vivid and she felt quite awake at the time.'

And interestingly, when Margaret Bradley visited a psychic some 16 years later, she was surprised to be told by him that she had 'heard spirit'. Not thinking of the voice she had heard, Margaret corrected him by saying that she had not. To which the psychic replied, 'Yes, you have. They are telling me that you have heard your name called.' He then added that the caller had been her deceased grandmother. But remarkable though this psychic impression was, it was probably wrong about the identity of the voice. For neither Margaret nor her mother recognized it, whereas they would have had no trouble in identifying Margaret's grandmother's voice, particularly as she had spoken with a strong Liverpool accent.

The most dramatic disembodied warning voices are those heard by soldiers, sailors and airmen in wartime, which save their lives, often by telling them to move from the spot where they are standing, moments before a bullet is fired or a bomb or shell explodes. Indeed, Margaret Gordon Moore mentions one flier whose life was thrice saved by a warning voice. She writes: 'One man said, "On three occasions I was directed by a clear voice to perform operations I would not have dreamed of, and each time they were successful and the course I had decided upon could only have proved fatal in my case, as it was to those who actually tried it".'

Many years ago I met a Korean gold-miner in Canada named Yung Bum Whang who told me that during the Korean War one of his uncles, who was serving in the South Korean Navy, had been saved from certain death by a warning voice. His ship had come under Communist shell-fire while sailing in East Korea Bay, and he had been knocked down and stunned when the vessel was hit. But as he came round he heard an unknown disembodied voice say urgently to him, 'Quick, move to the other side of the ship!' He struggled to his feet and with some difficulty did as the voice ordered. Then seconds later, a shell struck the deck where he had been lying and exploded. Without doubt Yung Bum Whang's uncle would have been killed but for the timely warning he received.

Another friend who was saved by a warning voice was the late Donald Styche, who during the Second World War served as a wireless operator on several merchant vessels. In early June 1942 he crossed the Atlantic aboard a small cargo ship carrying coal named the *Frederica Lensen*. The vessel docked first at Sydney, Nova Scotia, and then, after having taken aboard fresh supplies, she steamed into the St Lawrence estuary, heading for Montreal. But on 20 July she was torpedoed.

The explosion occurred inside the engine room of the *Frederica Lensen* at 12.30 p.m., causing the bunkers to collapse, the boilers to burst, and the ship to split in two at deck level. Donald told me: 'The explosion blew away the lifeboat outside the wireless room, where I would normally be passing at 12.30 p.m.' Yet on that particular day, having been instructed, to his astonishment, by a disembodied voice to go to the radio room half an hour early, and thus prematurely to relieve the other operator, he was fortunate to avoid being killed or seriously injured by the blast. 'It was a lucky escape,' Donald said modestly, adding: 'The ship wallowed but did not sink until about 5 hours later. Our escorts used depth charges and I believe got the submarine.'

Yet while Donald was thus saved by an unknown disembodied voice, which again was perhaps that of his daimonion, it must be wondered why the four men who worked in the engine room of the *Frederica Lensen* were not apprised of the danger by theirs. They were unfortunately all killed when the torpedo exploded. However, this may be explained by the fact that they had together reached their destined moment of death, whereas Donald Styche had not, which was why his life was preserved.

A remarkable escape from death resulting from a timely warning given by a disembodied voice happened in 1915 to a young Austrian soldier, a messenger in the 16th Bavarian Reserve Infantry Regiment. The following is an account of the incident that he gave to Ward Price, an English war correspondent, many years later:

I was eating my dinner in a trench with several comrades. Suddenly a voice seemed to be saying to me, 'Get up and go over there.' It was so clear and insistent that I obeyed mechanically, as if it had been a military order. I rose at once to my feet and walked twenty yards along the trench, carrying my dinner in its tin-can with me. Then I sat down to go on eating, my mind being once more at rest. Hardly had I done so when a flash and a deafening report came from the part of the trench I had just left. A stray shell had burst over the group in which I had been sitting, and every member was killed.

Hence the young man was saved in a nick of time from a stray shell blast by that helpful voice, whereas some twenty other men were killed. Yet while the voice had acted entirely benignly from his point of view, it was none the less perhaps the most malignant disembodied saviour in history. For the young soldier thus preserved was none other than Adolf Hitler, who went on to found the Nazi party in Germany and to start a war that caused the deaths of about 50 million people. This fact alone suggests that those ancient philosophers who believed that each of us has a good and an evil daimonion were probably right, and that it was young Hitler's evil daimonion that preserved him. Indeed, it is no exaggeration to say that that singular event changed the whole course of history in the twentieth century and with it the lives of countless millions of people. We are still living with its effects today.

But just as incredibly, a warning voice also saved Winston Churchill from serious injury or possibly death many years later. This close call happened one night during the Second World War, when Churchill, as part of his morale-boosting activities, was out visiting anti-aircraft batteries, to which he was driven by car. However, when he returned to his car from one battery, he strangely ignored the door being held open for him and instead walked around the vehicle and got in the other side. 'Something said "Stop!" before I reached the car door held open for me,' he recalled later. 'It then appeared to me that I was told I was meant to open the door on the other side and get in and sit there – and that's what I did.'

Not long afterwards, as the vehicle drove to the next battery through the darkened London streets, a bomb fell near the car, the blast lifting it up on to two wheels and nearly overturning it. Yet some deft driving by the chauffeur kept the car on the road, and Churchill's extra weight on the side lifted up helped to bring it safely down again on four wheels. A serious accident was thereby avoided.

Thus in this instance Winston Churchill was preserved at a time when England needed him most, which suggests the intelligence that spoke was aware of the danger to him and accordingly intervened on his behalf. Yet oddly, it did not always do so, for some years before, on 13 December 1931, when on a visit to New York, Churchill was struck by a taxi while exiting from the taxi which had brought him to Fifth Avenue. He was thrown into the air and received serious, but non-fatal injuries to the head, chest and thighs, which left him an invalid for two months. No helpful voice warned him on that occasion to watch what he was doing!

Another amazing escape from seemingly certain death, which was brought about by a disembodied warning voice, also happened during the Second World War. The person thus saved was a young American woman named Evelyn Horton. At the time she was employed as a statistician at a New Jersey aeroplane plant, working in a makeshift tin shack on the busy site. One day when she returned from lunch and passed a building under construction, a crane swung a heavy load of planks held in a chain sling directly over her. At that moment one of the chains slipped and the planks came tumbling out. 'The workmen yelled – but there was no time for anyone to do anything,' she later told Hereward Carrington. 'My first impulse was to run – no matter in what direction – just run. Then something within me said, "Do not move! Stand still and you will be safe." I remained motionless, my arms at my sides.'

Seconds later the planks crashed down like spilt matches all around Evelyn Horton, some tipping over on to the roofs of parked cars, others into nearby machinery, and some into workers who were seemingly standing at a safe distance. Yet miraculously, not one of them struck her. 'When the last board landed I looked about me,' she said. 'There was not the space of an inch between those boards and my feet. If I had moved in any direction I would have been struck. If I had stretched

out my arm to ward them off I would have had it broken. . . .
My little "hunch", as I called it then, had saved my life.'

This case is made particularly interesting by the fact that
the time between Evelyn Horton's awareness of the danger
posed by the falling planks and them landing around her was
extremely short, amounting to no more than a few seconds,
and because their final position was impossible to predict by
normal means. This indicates that she would have been unable
to 'intuit' that she must remain immobile; rather, the incident
seems to suggest that some intelligence with a forward exten-
sion in time and thus a knowledge of future spatial relation-
ships spoke to her, and that this was most likely to have been
her daimonion, whose warning was similar to those uttered
by the daimonion of Socrates.

One eleventh-century churchman was less fortunate than
Evelyn Horton because the disembodied voice he heard,
while warning him of his coming end, did not tell him how to
avoid the falling beam that killed him. The ill-fated prelate
was Bruno, the greedy, ambitious bishop of the German city
of Herbipolitanum (now Würzburg), who one day in about
1050 sailed down the Danube river with Henry III (1017–56),
emperor of Germany, when all aboard suddenly heard, upon
reaching a part of the river called Ben Strudel, near the
Austrian border, the loud cry: 'Ahoy! Ahoy! Bishop Bruno,
where are you travelling? But carry on as you wish, you shall
be my prey and victim.' Everyone was stunned by the
ominous words, and hurriedly crossed and blessed themselves, fearing they were addressed by an evil spirit. Robert
Southey poetically expresses the moment in the following
way:

> So he went on stately and proud,
> When he heard a voice that cried aloud,
> Ho! Ho! bishop Bruno! You travel with glee –
> But I would have you know, you travel to me!
>
> Behind, and before, on either side,
> He look'd, but nobody he espied;

> And the bishop at that grew cold with fear,
> For he heard the words distinct and clear.

Not long afterwards the bishop attended a feast given by Emperor Henry at a castle belonging to the Countess of Esburch, during which, according to Southey, the voice spoke to him again:

> And now the bishop had blest the meat,
> When a voice was heard as he sat in his seat,
> With the emperor now you are dining in glee,
> But know, bishop Bruno, you sup with me!

Yet while this disembodied announcement depressed the bishop's spirits, he did not stay down for long. The good food and wine, and the entertainments provided by the clowns and masquers, soon had him laughing again. But the voice spoke once more:

> Then from amid the masquers' crowd
> There went a voice hollow and loud;
> You have passed the day, bishop Bruno, with glee!
> But you must pass the night with me!

And suddenly, a rafter loosed itself from the roof of the dining hall and fell on Bishop Bruno as he sat at the festive table, killing him instantly. His sad end yet stands as a caution to all who besmirch their office and their religion with pride, haughtiness and greed.

But while all of the above-mentioned warnings were given by anonymous disembodied voices, there are occasions when the warning voice is recognized as belonging to someone known to the hearer, and who typically is no longer alive.

For example, Louisa Rhine reports that on blustery Labour Day (6 September) 1920, when a young female visitor to Niagara Falls was about to embark on the boat named *Maid of the Mist*, which carries tourists out into the spray, she was warned not to step on to the vessel by the voice of her dead

The author at age 19, shortly after he had been told by a disembodied voice that he did not have to fall for the girls he dated. He took the advice and became somewhat heartless, until he realized that he had been taught a profound lesson about the importance of love

Dan Slatter was as surprised as his two co-workers when an unknown disembodied voice called out the name of one of them. Unhappily the voice turned out to be a dire omen for the man concerned, who not long afterwards was diagnosed as having cancer of the spine

A week after her husband died, desperately unhappy Dorothy Wratten heard his voice call out her name in the same abrupt tone he had used in life when he was annoyed with her. This told her that he wanted her to get a grip on herself and learn to accept what had happened

The day before 19-year-old Jean Akerman was due to have a major operation, she went into the church beside the London hospital to pray for God's help. Then a wonderful voice told her that all would be well and she was not to be afraid, which proved both true and comforting

One Friday, Jeff Warlock heard an unknown disembodied voice tell him that his car would be stolen. He was so nonplussed by the voice that he failed to heed its warning. That night suspected joy-riders took the vehicle, although it was later found undamaged, as the voice had also predicted

After her son's tragic death, Jean Woodbridge not only had to cope with her grief but found her relationship with her husband deteriorating. Then a helpful disembodied voice informed her that as neither of them had the experience to cope, they should be less hard on themselves

When Jesus took Peter, James and John, three of the disciples, to the top of a high mountain, the latter not only saw Jesus being greeted by Moses and Elijah but they heard God's voice announce that Jesus was His son in whom He was well pleased, and that they should listen to him

This seal bears the only known portrait of Abbot Samson, the twelfth-century churchman whose life, and those of his companions, was saved when a disembodied voice roused him from sleep in time to snuff out a candle that was about to set fire to the straw of their sleeping quarters

When Samuel Johnson, the great eighteenth-century lexicographer, moralist and conversationalist, was a student at Oxford he once heard his mother's voice call out his name, notwithstanding the fact that she was some seventy miles away at Lichfield, his birthplace, at the time

Having left his home to live in a wilderness south of Rome, St Benedict was saved from starvation by a priest who brought food to his lonely cave. The priest had been prompted to search for Benedict by an angry disembodied voice, which chided him as he was about to eat his Easter dinner

Lord Herbert of Cherbury, the noted seventeenth-century diplomat, swordsman and lover, upon completing his now-famous book *De Veritate*, asked God for a sign that He wished him to publish such a contentious work. And to Lord Herbert's delight, that sign was immediately given

Young Giovanni Bernadone heard a voice speak to him when he prayed for guidance before a crucifix in a ruined church at Assisi. Heeding its call, he went on to found an order of monks, known as the Franciscans, whose name derives from his childhood nickname of 'Francis'

sister, which clearly said 'Don't go, don't go!', and which sounded as if her sibling was standing right next to her. The voice was accompanied by the girl developing a sudden pain in her right arm and leg, which effectively paralysed her and which lasted until the boat had left the shore.

Yet while both the voice and the paralysis might possibly have been produced by the girl's own anxiety about the imagined dangers of the short voyage, she did not in fact report feeling any anxiety beforehand. Moreover, the vessel came back soon afterwards bringing some passengers that had been injured when the mast toppled over in the strong wind. This was the first ever accident aboard the *Maid of the Mist*. The voice and the associated paralysis therefore saved the girl from injury or possibly even from death.

In another case reported by the same researcher, a young North Carolina woman named Harriet was saved from being run over, by the warning voice of her dead mother who had passed away when Harriet was only 12 years old. Oddly, when Harriet was out shopping one day, she was startled to notice a woman dressed in clothes identical to those once worn by her mother, whereby she exactly resembled her. The woman hurried along ahead of Harriet, and was soon lost from sight in the crowd. But not long afterwards, as Harriet was crossing the tram tracks running along Main Street, she heard her mother's voice shout warningly, 'Harriet, Harriet, look out!' Staring hurriedly round, Harriet saw a tram coming straight at her, and just had time to leap back out of its way. Her dead mother's call therefore saved her life.

The occurrence is made particularly perplexing by the near simultaneous appearance of Harriet's mother's look-alike. If this likeness was in fact her mother's wraith, then it obviously played a direct part in Harriet's brush with death, as she would clearly have been more attentive to her surroundings and to their dangers if she had not seen it. But if the woman was mortal and thus had only a coincidental likeness to her mother, her sudden appearance was enough to distract Harriet's attention, causing her to step on to the tram tracks as a tram was approaching, and thereby provoking her dead mother to warn her verbally of the danger from beyond the grave. If true, this naturally suggests that we are kept under close observation by loved ones who have predeceased us. And it seems that they will warn us, either vocally or in some other way, if our lives are in danger at any time before our fated moment of death.

5 The Prophetic Voice

Just as Cadwallader was preparing his fleet, an Angelic Voice spoke to him in a peal of thunder and told him to stop.... The Voice added that, as a reward for its faithfulness, the British people would occupy the island again at some time in the future, once the appointed moment should come.

From *The History of the Kings of Britain*
by Geoffrey of Monmouth

We have already noted that disembodied voices do sometimes predict the future, even though this foreknowledge is generally implied rather than made plain. Hence the hearer is usually told what to do, and is saved thereby from distress, injury or death, rather than being directly apprised of what is going to happen. This suggests that while the daimonion or intelligence behind the voice knows what is ahead, it is reluctant to state it openly. Only rarely does the voice, which is invariably unknown, speak of things to come in such a way that the hearer can gain some financial or worldly advantage from them, as happened to Mrs Margaret Gordon Moore, and also to her son Graeme, who was given the winner of a horse race scheduled for the following day.

This was equally true of earlier, pre-Christian times. Moreover, while pagans believed in omens and signs and they practised many different types of divination, the responses evoked seldom came in the form of an external disembodied voice; and even when the reply was vocal, it was usually uttered through a human intermediary, much like a modern spiritualist medium acts (or claims to act) as a mouthpiece for the dead.

91

Thus at Delphi, for example, the ancient world's most famous prophetic shrine, situated on Mount Parnassus in Greece, the god Apollo revealed the future to his specially trained attendant, the Pythia, who became sensitized to his words by breathing in the mephitic vapours emerging from the rocky floor of the subterranean *adyton* or oracular chamber. The dissociative effects of these natural fumes were later augmented by burning a mixture of hemp, barley grains and chopped bay-leaves on a tripod, which produced in the chamber an intoxicating yet noxious smoke containing potassium cyanide, and which, when inhaled, prompted divine revelations.

But while no external voice was heard by the seeker who accompanied the Pythia into the adyton, the Pythia herself was privy to an internal one – supposedly that of the god Apollo – which gave her an answer to the question asked. Thus she did not obtain the response by 'second sight' or precognition, or for that matter by inspired guesswork. Indeed, the answers given by the god were invariably accurate, despite often being somewhat ambiguous. Then, after Apollo's revelation to the Pythia, her inevitably rambling version of his oracular words was transformed into a short verse written by a literate helper, which was given to the awe-inspired seeker to take home with him.

However, there was one Greek shrine at which an external disembodied voice was heard. This occurred at the oracle dedicated to Trophonius, at Lebadeia in Boeotia. Trophonius was not a god, but he had been granted a shrine after death because he and his brother Agamedes had used their architectural skills in life to construct the first stone temple at Delphi, and because Apollo had afterwards granted them a quick, painless or divine death, which they had both desired, following a six-day period of riotous living. In fact it was their early demise that gave rise to the now-familiar saying 'Those whom the gods love, die young'.

The shrine of Trophonius is also interesting because it was not Trophonius's shade that spoke, but rather a minor deity known as the Good Daimonion, which seems to have been the *genius loci* of the underground chamber wherein its voice was heard. Also, those who sought its prophecies had to undergo a lengthy period of preparation and purification, which brought them a state of psychological readiness, and which was similar in many respects to that endured by young American Indians, who sought vocal guidance and assistance from a guardian spirit, as I shall discuss in the next chapter. We are fortunate in having a first-hand description of the various preliminaries required before a suppliant could be 'going to Trophonius', written by a second century AD seeker at the shrine named Pausanias, who included it in his famous *Guide to Greece*.

The preparatory activities took place in a sacred grove of trees flanking the river Herkyna, which flowed through a mountainous part of Boeotia near Lebadeia. Among the trees was a hostel dedicated to Good Fortune and to the Good Daimonion, wherein the suppliant stayed for a week or longer. While there he had to purify himself daily with cold baths in the river (hot water was eschewed), and his food consisted of meat cut from animal sacrifices made to Trophonius. The sacrifices were also important in determining the most propitious time to consult the Good Daimonion, which was done by inspecting the victim's entrails. The results obtained naturally governed the length of time he spent at the hostel.

When the omens were favourable, the suppliant was taken that night to the river Herkyna, accompanied by two teenage boys, known as Hermai, who bathed and anointed him. He was then led to two adjacent springs, one of which was called Lethe (or Forgetfulness), the other Mnemosyne (or Memory). By drinking from the first, he forgot all his previous worries and concerns, and by afterwards drinking from the second, he prepared his mind to remember all that was to come. He next prayed at the statue of Daedalus, the celebrated builder of the Cretan Labyrinth, following which he was given a special costume to wear, made up of a linen tunic, tied with ribbons, and heavy locally-made boots.

Thus clad, he was taken up to the oracular chamber on the mountainside above the sacred wood. The first part was a large, dome-shaped chasm in the ground, rather like an upturned flower pot, which was about 20-feet deep and 10-feet across at the base. By using a narrow, rickety ladder, the man 'going to Trophonius' entered the upper opening and climbed alone down into its murky interior, his heart doubtless pumping with fear, to reach the stone floor. On one side of the cavity, where the wall met the floor, was a pitch-dark aperture about two feet wide and one foot deep. This was the opening to the sacred *oraculum*. To gain entry, the suppliant had next to lie on his back on the floor, clutching a honey-cake in each hand, and push his feet and lower legs into the opening.

What happened next was staggering. The suppliant, to his amazement, was drawn swiftly into the oracular chamber, to find himself in total darkness. Indeed, it was as if he had died. His sudden movement thither was seemingly supernatural, for Pausanias says that it was 'as if some extraordinarily deep, fast river' caught him and pulled him through. Then crouching alone, disorientated and terrified in the pitch darkness, the shaking suppliant received the divine revelation for which he had come. This was either given to him in the form of a visionary experience, or as happened more often, he heard the disembodied voice of the Good Daimonion reveal what the future would bring to him. Then about half an hour later, stunned by what he had seen and/or heard, he was just as remarkably conveyed back into the first chamber. He eventually managed to climb back up to its opening, and so return to the familiar everyday world. After being interviewed by the shrine priests, who placed him in the Seat of Memory and to whom he recounted the revelations imparted to him, he was helped back to the hostel by his friends, and left alone to recover his senses fully. Because most suppliants returned from this ordeal looking pale and despondent, it became proverbial in the ancient world to describe anyone who was naturally of that appearance as having 'gone to Trophonius'.

For the modern cynic, who might regard the entry of the suppliant into the oracular chamber and the experiences he had therein, as being stage-managed by clever priests, it is important to point out that the oracle of Trophonius gained great renown throughout the ancient world, which could only have come about through the accuracy of its prophecies. And fortunately, we have some record of these and of the events which preceded them. Plutarch, for example, refers to the shrine in his biography of the famous Roman commander Lucius Cornelius Sylla (c. 138–78 BC), who drove out the army of Mithridates, king of Pontus, from Greece, and who fought two important battles against him in Boeotia, the first at Chaeronea (where, coincidentally, Plutarch was born), and the second at Orchomenus. Both towns lie close to Lebadeia, which gave some of Sylla's men the opportunity to visit the shrine of Trophonius after the first battle and to make enquiries about the future prospects of their commander. Plutarch writes of this:

Quintus Titius, a man of some note among the Romans employed in Greece, came to (Sylla) one day after he had gained the battle of Chaeronea, and told him, that Trophonius foretold another battle to be fought shortly in the same place, in which he should likewise prove victorious. After him, came a private soldier of his own, with a promise from heaven of the glorious success that would attend his affairs in Italy. Both agreed as to the manner in which these prophecies were communicated: they said, the deity that appeared to them, both in beauty and majesty resembled the Olympian Jupiter.

Both those prophecies came to pass. The successful battle at Orchomenus, as I mentioned above, followed that of Chaeronea, and Sylla afterwards returned with his army hurriedly to Rome, where he defeated Marius and his other enemies, and established himself as dictator. But alas, he made himself despicable by his perfidy and cruelty, although he had the grace to abdicate when he had restored order to the capital. He retired to Puteoli to write his commentaries, and died there in torment from an infestation of lice, aged 60.

However, we are regretfully left with no account of what Apollo's voice sounded like, or that of the Good Daimonion, which must therefore remain as enigmatic as the mellifluous singing of the Sirens. Yet we can perhaps be sure that they rivalled in beauty the unknown female voice heard by the bedridden J.D. Blackman, whose tones were 'the clearest, purest, sweetest that a mortal being can conceive. No human voice could equal it in its qualities'.

It was an 'Apollonine' inner voice that predicted the future to a Christian bishop in AD 418. The man was Amator, the bishop of Auxerre in Gaul, the town where the governor Germanus was wont to take hunting holidays from time to time with his wife Eustachia. However, Germanus upset Amator by hanging the dried carcasses of game animals in the branches of the fine old pear tree that grew in Auxerre's central square. To the bishop, this smacked too much of the heathen practice of decorating trees, and when Germanus refused to change his ways, Amator simply had the pear tree cut down. Germanus was furious when he learned what had been done, and he resolved to have Amator put to death.

The bishop made no effort to escape and said to those who urged him to flee, that his end was of no consequence, for he was happy to die for what he believed. However, even as he spoke those words, an inner voice told him that, while he would indeed soon die, it was not Germanus who would kill him, but on the contrary, the governor was destined to succeed him as bishop!

And to everyone's amazement, this is what happened. Governor Germanus had a change of mind about putting Amator to death, whereupon Amator not only recommended Germanus's appointment as bishop to the Prefect, but on the very day that he was destined to die – 1 May 418 – he invited Germanus to his church, locked the door to prevent his escape, and then carried out a hasty investiture before the startled governor could stop him. Later that day, while sitting on the Bishop's Throne, Amator collapsed and died, and Germanus in due course accepted the post so surprisingly thrust upon him. He was bishop for thirty years, becoming 'reverenced throughout the empire for his wisdom and holiness'. And he spent the years 429–30 and 447 in Britain combating outbreaks of the Pelagian heresy, which maintained that there is no such thing as Original Sin. Bishop Germanus died in July 448.

Where ambiguous prophecies are concerned, we must take note of the one, recorded by William of Newburgh, that was given by a disembodied voice to Stephen, the governor of Anjou. It spoke through the brazen head owned by a Toledo diviner, whom Stephen consulted in 1193, shortly after his royal master, King Richard I, had been captured and imprisoned by the German Emperor Henry VI. The news of his capture gladdened Stephen, who had exceeded his powers while Richard was away in the Holy Land and who feared punishment when he returned. He therefore wanted to know if that would happen.

The diviner told Stephen that he might ask three questions, but that they should be short and to the point. Stephen therefore inquired of the head if he would ever see King Richard again, to which the voice, booming out from its brazen surroundings, replied 'No!' He then asked how long his administration would last, and was told that it would continue until his death. And finally, he inquired where he would die, and was told 'In pluma' – which in translation meant, or so Stephen supposed, 'in feathers'. The corrupt administrator then went away much relieved and very pleased by what he had heard, believing that his position was safe, if not unassailable, and that he would live for as long as he stayed clear of feathers. He therefore ordered that anything filled with feathers, or covered with feathers, in his house and domain should be destroyed. It was bad news for his ducks, hens and geese, of course, as they were all killed, and tough on the feather mattress and down pillow makers. And once that had all been done, Stephen conducted himself more arrogantly and heavy-handedly than ever.

In fact, Stephen made himself particularly unpleasant to one individual noble, who had earlier criticized his behaviour and whom he suspected of having complained about him to the king. Stephen in fact gathered together an army and went in search of the man, intending to punish him for his disloyalty. This obliged the noble, whose forces were outnumbered, to flee to one of his castles for refuge. Stephen, however, quickly surrounded it, confident that it would only be a matter of time before the man surrendered. But desperation made the noble attempt a daring kidnap, which he carried out when Stephen rode around the castle to ascertain which part was most vulnerable to attack. As he passed the postern gate, the noble and his men sallied forth, killed Stephen's retainers, and captured the governor. Praising God, the noble carried Stephen into the castle, and although Stephen begged for mercy and offered a large ransom for his release, the noble told him that now he was in Pluma, for that was the name of his castle, he would never escape. He then had the governor cruelly tortured and killed, as a traitor to his king and his country.

As I related in Chapter Three, the Buckinghamshire vicar Dr Richard Napier was often spoken to by a disembodied voice, which he believed belonged to the angel Raphael. It regularly prophesied to him whether or not his medical patients would survive their afflictions, and if they were destined to, it would pass on to the doctor a suitable remedy.

However, Raphael's voice would sometimes make more general predictions. In 1621, for example, it foretold that John Prideaux would become a bishop in twenty years time, and indeed in 1641 he was actually made Bishop of Worcester. His son Humphrey (born 1648) followed him into the Church, becoming one of its best-known historians. Likewise, the angelic voice predicted in 1619 that a Cheshire gentleman named Booth would have a son three years later, who would become his heir, which was fulfilled when a male child, whom he christened George, was born to his spouse on 18 December 1622. 'It is impossible that the prediction of Sir George

Booth's birth,' comments John Aubrey, 'could be found any other way, but by angelic revelation.'

A startling prophecy of a coming earthquake was given twice by a disembodied voice to a 26-year-old Canadian Indian squaw. The surprising event is recorded in the 1663 *Relation de la Nouvelles-France* or *Narrative of New France*, wherein the woman reports:

On the night of the 4th or 5th of February, in the year 1663, being perfectly awake, and in sound judgement, and setting up as it were in my bed, I heard a distinct and intelligible voice, that said to me 'There will happen today many strange things. The earth will quake and tremble'. I found myself seized with an extraordinary fear, because I saw no person from whom the voice could proceed. I, full of terror, with great difficulty, endeavoured to compose myself to sleep. As soon as it was day I told my husband what had happened to me. About nine or ten of the clock the same day, going to a forest awood-gathering, I was scarce got into the brow of the forest, but I heard the same voice again, which told me the same thing. My fear was much greater because I was all alone.

The frightened squaw hurriedly finished collecting an armful of wood and then made for home. On the way she met her sister, to whom she related what had happened, and she also repeated it to her father when she arrived back. Hence like her husband, both heard about the voice's warning of the coming earthquake, yet none of them entirely believed her, dismissing her story as fanciful. However, they all experienced its truth when later that same day, between about 5 and 6 o'clock in the afternoon, an earthquake struck the region and caused much damage and loss of life, particularly in the isolated French settlements.

Another prophecy made by an external voice, which was told to Aubrey by 'my worthy friend and old acquaintance Thomas Marriet of Warwickshire', is included in the former's *Miscellanies Upon Various Subjects*. Yet it concerned an event of a relatively minor importance.

The incident happened to a doctor named Smith, of

Tamworth in Warwickshire, in about 1685. Apparently Mr Smith – 'an understanding sober person' – was in bed one evening perusing a copy of Raphael Holinshed's *Chronicles* (1577), upon which Shakespeare had based several of his plays, and he was greatly interested to read therein an account of the battle fought between the Celtic king, Vortigern and the Angle king, Hengest, not least because it took place at nearby Colemore. Soon afterwards, having put down the book in order to go to sleep, Mr Smith was greatly surprised to hear an unknown disembodied voice suddenly say, 'You shall shortly see some of the bones of those men and horses slain, that you read of.' Hurriedly sitting up and calling out to ask who in the name of God spoke to him, the voice replied that he need not trouble himself about that, but should only remember that what it had said would soon happen.

And indeed the mysterious voice turned out to be correct (or apparently so), for not long afterwards, when paying a visit to a neighbour named Colonel Archer, Mr Smith was amazed to discover that the Colonel's servants, while digging for marl to use as fertilizer, had by accident uncovered an ancient battlefield. On being shown the archaeological finds, which included numerous skeletons of men and horses, along with weapons and potsherds, Mr Smith could not help but notice that the remains closely matched the description of the battle in Holinshed's *Chronicles*. Thus as far as Mr Smith could tell, the disembodied voice had accurately predicted what he would see.

But while the story is impressive, the historical facts do not match those of the *Chronicles* as Aubrey relates them. A battle between Vortigern and Hengest did take place in AD 455, but it was fought at Aylesford in Kent, not at Colemore in Warwickshire, which in fact, I believe, does not exist. Thus if an ancient battlefield was accidentally uncovered by Colonel Archer's workmen near Tamworth, it was not the site of that fought between Vortigern and Hengest. Hence while the voice was right about the archaeological find, it was wrong about the combatants.

A grim and true prediction which came from the hearing of two disembodied voices, was implicit in their sound rather than in what they said. Hence the voices were omens of the fatalities signified. The incident happened on the Isle of Skye in about 1765, and it was recorded by James Boswell in his estimable *Journal of a Tour to the Hebrides* (1785). Apparently, when a local laird named Kingsburgh was out riding one day, he passed a group of farm women excitably talking together in a field beside the road. On hailing them, they explained that 'they had heard two *taiscks*, (that is, two voices of persons about to die) and what was remarkable, one of them was an *English taisck*, which they never heard before.'

At that early date the natives of those remote Scottish islands spoke only Erse, which explains why the hearing of a spirit talking in English was noteworthy to the women. The significance of the *taiscks* became apparent to Mr Kingsburgh when he eventually rode back along the same track, for he encountered two funerals at the very place where he had chanced upon the fieldworkers, one of which 'was that of a woman who had come from the mainland, and could speak only English.'

The event is of particular interest to us because it is an instance of several people hearing two disembodied voices at the same time, which happens but rarely. It is a pity that Mr Kingsburgh's daughter, who was Boswell's source, does not mention if what the voices said was discernible or that of one understandable, or whether only their sound was heard. Indeed, it is curious that some disembodied voices cannot be understood, despite the fact that they are speaking in the language of the hearer, although as I mentioned earlier this can happen for a number of reasons. The shock of a sudden vocal pronouncement may result in the hearer losing the words, or the sheer speed of the utterance may render it unintelligible.

Two recent examples of such content loss are worth recording here. When the psychic Eileen Landau died at 12.30 p.m. on 28 December 1996, her husband Lucian, who was at her bedside, reported: 'At that moment I heard at least three [disembodied] voices speaking together in a very excited manner. My impression was that it was a kind of welcoming party, but unfortunately I could not catch a single word as they were all talking at the same time.' And Renée Hayes, writing in *The Seeing Eye, The Seeing I*, recounts how a woman nursing the terminally ill daughter of the owner of a country house, which stood in a very sequestered spot, suddenly:

heard music outside the windows. It was like voices singing, she said, but the words were indistinguishable, and the whole thing struck her as 'strange, different, on another wave length'. There was no one outside, no one in the house was playing a record or a radio, and there was no accounting for the sound. The dying girl heard it too, and said, 'They are coming for me, I must go soon.' Late next morning she was gone.

In about 1920, the French traveller Alexandra David-Neel visited the monastery at Podang, in Sikkim, northern India. While she was there, the new maharajah-lama also arrived for a short stay. He was brought thither by his concern about the superstitions of the local hill farmers, who drank alcohol, sacrificed animals and worshipped spirits, and to combat such pernicious practices he had asked an Indian monk named Kali Kumar to tour the area and to preach the strict rules of orthodox Buddhism to them. But that afternoon, when Alexandra David-Neel was taking tea with the maharajah-lama and talking over the possible success of Kali Kumar's mission, she was suddenly interrupted by an unseen presence, which spoke to her:

'Nothing you can do will succeed,' said a soundless voice. 'The people of this country are mine . . . I am more powerful than you. . . .'
I listened in amazement to these silent words, and I had almost decided that they were only the expression of my own doubts regarding the success of the proposed reforms, when the maharajah replied.

He replied to that which I had not said, arguing with the invisible adversary of his plans. 'Why should I not succeed?' he went on to say. 'Possibly it will take some time to change the ideas of the peasants and the lower clergy. The demons which they feed will not easily become resigned to die of hunger, but, nevertheless, I shall get the better of them. . . .'

But alas, the maharajah-lama was wrong. The religious reforms begun by him were shortly afterwards terminated by his unexpected death. Kali Kumar's mission and his preaching were therefore stopped and the hill farmers quickly reverted to their former quasi-heathen ways. 'The invisible adversary triumphed,' comments Mrs David-Neel, 'as he had predicted he would.'

An invisible entity of a different kind spoke to a 7-year-old boy named Ray Logan one day in 1934 as he stood looking out of a window of his parents' first-floor flat in Sunderland, County Durham. The schoolboy was sick with a contagious skin complaint and he was all alone in the house. Then suddenly, as he watched the traffic go by and anxiously wondered what the future held for him, Ray heard to his astonishment a very loud, beautifully modulated, but commanding voice within the room say to him: 'Do not worry, Ray. It does not matter what you do for the rest of your life. The important time is much later – 55!'

Ray had no idea where the voice had come from or why it had spoken to him, and he was not helped in this regard by his parents, who merely smiled when he told them about his experience and went on to talk about other things. For they, like most parents faced with such a strange report, thought he was making it up. The voice was therefore ignored and, as it did not recur, Ray gradually forgot about it. The years passed and Ray grew up. He joined the Royal Navy and later served in the mercantile marine. When he came ashore he had a variety of jobs including that of a cartoonist. But disappointingly, 1955 came and went without any further contact. Not long afterwards, at age 32, Ray became a chauffeur for a hire car

· DISEMBODIED VOICES ·

company operating out of Gatwick Airport. He greatly enjoyed this job and began to feel settled in life. Then in 1981 he reached the grand old age of 55.

Two weeks after his birthday, as promised and predicted, the same voice spoke to him again. Its vocalization coincided with Ray losing something of great personal value, which he had searched high and low for without success. Then from out of the blue, the voice told him where to look. He followed its instructions and located what he was seeking. More help was forthcoming, as soon afterwards, having picked up two Italians in his taxi at Gatwick Airport who spoke no English, he found the only clue to their destination that they possessed was a piece of paper with the words 'York Hotel' written on it. Ray had no idea where the hotel was, or even if it was in London, but the helpful voice came to his rescue. 'Do not worry, Ray,' it said comfortingly. 'We will help you find the York Hotel.' And without hesitation it directed him into London and then through the city streets to the right place. 'I swear it was like listening to a London policeman,' recalls Ray. 'Except for the perfection of the English!'

Since then Ray, now a Brighton resident, has had many communications from the voice. However, this is where we must leave him, for the voice is not that of his daimonion or spirit guide, but instead it claims to come from an extraterrestrial intelligence, one of several known as the 'Overlords'. Apparently hailing from a distant galaxy, these alien beings have told Ray much about all manner of things, including civilization, UFOs, GM foods, AIDS, mythology, computers, the pyramids, Atlantis, druids, magnetic locomotion, space flight, anti-matter, doomsday, and how they genetically bred us humans from gorillas, which he has collected together into a book entitled *The Sirius Papers*. Yet while the Overlords are voluble, they are not particularly original or insightful, although this may simply be because they are a long way from home.

In the early summer of 1998, a 41–year-old computer programmer named Jeff Warlock was forewarned by a disembodied voice of a distressing event that was about to happen to him. The singular announcement, which surprised him greatly, occurred one Friday at Bacup in Lancashire. At about 7.45 p.m. on the evening in question, Jeff arrived by car outside a woman friend's house, where he was invited to stay for the weekend, only to find that all the parking places were occupied. However, he finally managed to locate an empty bay standing in an isolated spot about 60 yards past her house. It was when he had parked there that the voice spoke to him:

As I turned off the ignition a voice, female I think, spoke loudly and clearly in my right ear: 'Your car will be stolen but it'll be all right. You'll get it back.' Stunned, I spent the next few minutes on automatic pilot, unloading the car, putting the radio in the boot and going over to my friend's house. Sure enough the next morning [Saturday] the car was gone. The police recovered it late that afternoon. It was damaged, the door had been damaged, the steering lock smashed and there was some sill damage, indicating that it had been taken by joy-riders and raced but otherwise it was fine.

The voice that uttered the prophecy, Jeff told me, was unknown to him, which suggests that it might have belonged to his daimonion, although he had never heard it speak to him before and has not done so since. That the voice was not an expression of his own fear that his car might be stolen, is indicated by the fact that it was entirely correct in telling him that the vehicle would be found in relatively good condition. For Jeff would naturally have assumed that if his car was stolen it would either not be recovered or, if it was, it would be badly damaged, perhaps beyond repair. And while we may wonder why Jeff did not respond to the voice's warning and move his car to a more secure location, his lack of action is entirely understandable when it is remembered that the voice was a completely unusual and unexpected phenomenon and thus seemed to be of more importance than the possible theft of his car. Furthermore, because such mental events are commonly regarded as hallucinations, Jeff Warlock had no reason to accord the voice any more authority than he did his own anxiety.

Although I have written mainly about people who have heard a disembodied voice only once or twice in their lives, which I have done to separate my subjects from those who are perhaps suffering (or are considered to be suffering) from a mental disorder, there is one case of a voice being often heard that deserves mention here. Indeed, the case bears some striking parallels to that of Socrates, who, as we have noted, was accompanied throughout his life by a daimonion, or invisible spirit guide, which not only counselled him to do what was right and which protected him from harm, but which would, when necessary, urge him to advise others in a similar way.

The middle-aged woman concerned, whom I shall call Elizabeth to protect her identity, is a resident of Malvern, in Worcestershire. The voice that she hears, which she regards, being a devout Christian, as belonging to her guardian angel, began speaking to her when she was a child, as did the daimonion of Socrates. She told me: 'I have had an invisible companion since I was seven years old and its voice has educated, informed, comforted and advised me all of my life. It has told me things past, present, and future. . . . It guides me in every important event and *it is never wrong*. I trust it implicitly.'

Elizabeth says that she hears her 'angel's voice' internally and that it is quite distinct from her own thoughts. It is neither male nor female in tone and it has no accent. It also has, as we would expect, an identity and independence separate from that of herself. 'My inner voice speaks when it wishes,' she says, adding, 'If I am stupid it frequently scolds me. . . . It is very strict and moral and frequently tells me where I am going wrong – should I disobey I certainly have to face the consequences.'

In this regard the intelligence behind the voice therefore functions as an entirely benign guardian, which furthermore, Elizabeth adds, 'often warns me to be careful of my speech and/or my opinions.' Yet none the less, although she often talks to her 'angel', she never asks it about itself, believing that its origin and purpose are none of her business. And should she disobey what it tells her to do, she is reprimanded by having her plans go wrong or by things going astray.

When Elizabeth was pregnant the voice informed her that she was carrying twins, although nobody believed her until she had a scan and the fact was verified. And when her husband unknowingly developed a fatal illness, the voice informed her of this and predicted its inevitable outcome:

I was told of my husband's illness months before it became apparent and I knew quite surely he was going to die. It is very hard to maintain a cheerful manner for the sake of the family when one knows that the dearest person on earth is about to leave and I don't really understand how I got through it. . . . I begged him so often to see a doctor and he always laughed at me, saying I was not to fuss as he felt completely well. I asked him to take more care of himself and suggested many ways but he said none of it was necessary, and I could not compel him. If you have ever tried to tell a loved one that they have a life-threatening disease, and tried to do so without scaring them unduly, you will know what I was up against.

Elizabeth's voice also informed her of Princess Diana's death two weeks before the dreadful event happened. She has similarly been told when other people are going to die. Yet she is quite adamant that when the voice gives her such information, she is forbidden from informing the person concerned that his or her demise is imminent. Indeed, she believes that her 'angel' would leave her if she did.

But while her 'angel's voice' may seem to be a rather restrictive, not to say gloomy, companion to have, Elizabeth does find reassurance in the fact that it laughs a lot. She cannot, she admits, explain it, but she believes that it comes from God and is grateful for its presence, although she quite understandably says, 'I keep quiet about it generally as I have no wish to be regarded as a lunatic by my neighbours!'

6   Miscellaneous Voices and Other Sounds

> Then by some secret shrine I ride;
> I hear a voice, but none are there;
> The stalls are void, the doors are wide,
> The tapers burning fair.
> > From *Sir Galahad* by Alfred Lord Tennyson

In addition to the known or unknown disembodied voices considered earlier, which either call out a name or say a sentence of advice, or give a warning or a prophecy, there are those that do not fit neatly into any of these categories. This may be due to the nature of what is said, or to the fact that the words cannot be understood, or occasionally because the sound itself is not a vocal expression. Such anomalous pronouncements and noises are the subject of this chapter.

One of the most remarkable examples of a variety of disembodied sounds, which included that of numerous voices, is recorded in *II Kings*, Chapter VII of the Old Testament.

In about the year 892 BC the city of Samaria was besieged by the Syrian king Ben-Hadad I. When the food supplies ran out, starvation ensued and some Samaritans were even driven by hunger to eat their own children. This led the four desperate lepers who begged for food at the city's gate to decide to improve their chances of survival by throwing themselves on the mercy of the Syrians, who they knew would either kill them or, as they hoped, feed them! Early next morning they therefore went to the Syrian camp, where they were astounded to find that the enemy had all gone, leaving behind virtually everything they had brought with them. And the reason for the Syrians' surprising and hurried departure was almost beyond belief:

For the Lord made the host of the Syrians to hear a noise of chariots, and a noise of horses, *even* the noise of a great host: and they said one to another, Lo, the king of Israel hath hired against us the kings of the Hittites, and the kings of the Egyptians, to come against us. Wherefore they arose and fled in the twilight, and left their tents, and their horses, and their asses, even the camp as it *was*, and flew for their life.

The king of Israel had of course hired neither the Hittites nor the Egyptians, and neither had he made any advance upon the Syrians himself. The Syrian host, which probably numbered about 20,000 men, was thus reacting to the disembodied sounds of a non-existent approaching army that were somehow *just there!* These were not only mistaken for the real thing by trained soldiers, but were loud enough to appear to belong to a superior force. And clearly, only a real fear for their lives would explain why the Syrians fled in panic without either breaking camp or taking their pack animals and other belongings with them.

Something similar happened in 479 BC when the Persians led by Xerxes (or 'Warrior') invaded Greece. On marching to the town of Delphi, where the god Apollo had his oracle, several negative omens occurred. These included a fall of thunderbolts from the sky and the tumbling down of two rocky peaks from Mount Parnassus, which fell among the Persians and killed many of them. But most alarming of all was the loud disembodied voice that shouted angrily at them from within Apollo's shrine, and which caused the Persians to flee in terror.

Later that same year, numerous disembodied singing voices were heard shortly before the sea battle at Salamis, when the

Persian fleet was destroyed. The witnesses were two Greek soldiers, named Demaratus and Dicaeus, who were escaping through the plain of Thriasia following the Persian army's victory in Attica. They first saw a long cloud of dust, such as might be raised by an army of 30,000 soldiers, blowing towards Salamis, and then heard the sound of voices ululating the holy Iacchus song, which was only chanted at nearby Eleusis during the mysteries of Dionysius. The two men knew that both manifestations were divine in origin, not least because the whole of Attica had been cleared of its inhabitants by the Persian army. They therefore concluded that Xerxes was destined to be defeated at Salamis, which proved to be true.

Pliny records that during the war with the barbarian Cimbri and Teutones tribes, who invaded the Roman empire in considerable numbers at the close of the second century BC, the sound of clashing arms and the blast of trumpets were heard in the air, which rightly dismayed the Romans, who suffered several defeats at the barbarians' hands. Later on, in 84 BC when Cornelius Sylla was considering returning to Rome, Plutarch says that 'one day when the sky was serene and clear, there was heard in it the sound of a trumpet, so loud, so shrill and mournful, that it frightened and astonished the whole world'. The omen, however, was given a positive interpretation by Sylla's Tuscan sages and his return to the capital, as we have already seen, was to his advantage.

Another ancient case of a disembodied voice heard by many happened in the early years of the first century AD. The event was recorded by Plutarch, to whom it was told by Epitherses, his former schoolmaster at Chaeronea, who was present on the occasion. Epitherses said that while he was taking a voyage to Italy, his vessel was becalmed one evening off two small islands known as the Paxoi, which lie between Corcyra (modern Corfu) and Leucas in the Ionian Sea. Suddenly a voice was heard shouting as if from on shore, calling to Thamus, the Egyptian pilot on board, who would not answer it until he had been addressed for a third time. Having then responded, the mysterious voice said to him, 'Thamus, when you come to Palodes, proclaim it aloud, that the great god Pan is dead!' Everyone on the ship heard the announcement and all were amazed by it, for the death of a god had never been publically revealed before. And Thamus, when the island of Palodes was reached, stood on the ship's stern and loudly repeated the dreadful news to those ashore. This brought answering shrieks of despair, which were quickly followed by the sounds of lamentation. And it is said that when the Roman emperor Tiberius, who ruled from AD 14 to 37, heard of the remarkable occurrence, he sent for Thamus and was assured by him that it had actually taken place.

However, the poet and classical scholar Robert Graves, writing in *The Greek Myths*, comments that 'The Egyptian Thamus apparently misheard the ceremonial lament *Thamus Pan-megas Tethnece* ("the all-great Tammuz is dead!") for the message: "Thamus, Great Pan is dead!" ' But this interpretation is doubtful. Tammuz, after all, was a Mesopotamian vegetation god, who, like Demeter, departed for the underworld each autumn, which makes a ceremonial mourning for him on a small and remote Greek island an extremely unlikely happening. Furthermore, Thamus the Egyptian pilot was not the only person who heard the call. The Greek passengers, one of whom was Epitherses, all confirmed what had been shouted in Greek about Pan. They would surely have corrected Thamus had he been mistaken about this.

The vocal announcement of Pan's death also accords with what was believed about the god. Pan, a son of Hermes, was a mysterious deity, half-human, half-animal, having the legs and horns of a goat and a sex-urge that was similarly caprine. He habitually lived in rural Arcadia, and he was worshipped as the divine guardian of flocks, herds, and beehives. On warm summer afternoons Pan's favourite pastime was sleeping in some grotto or cave, and if any passers-by inadvertently woke him, he would terrify them with a loud shout, sending them running off, as we still say, in *pan*ic.

Moreover, Pausanias records that, in about 490 BC, Pan was heard singing a paean or song of praise, which was written by the lyric poet Pindar (*c.* 522–443 BC), at a remote spot somewhere between Cithaeron and Helicon, two mountains in Boeotia. Pausanias also notes that Pindar, one of Greece's greatest artistic geniuses, composed a hymn of gratitude to Pan for performing his humble musical creation. But more in keeping with the traditional vocality of the god was the fearful cry that was said to have resounded through the air on 22 September 479 BC, when the Greeks engaged the Persians at the battle of Plataea, a town in Boeotia. The Persians were so alarmed by the sound that they fled in disorder from the battlefield, leaving the Greeks as victors, a defeat that brought an end to the Persian invasion. Indeed, because 'the Greeks attributed the unexpected disembodied cry to Pan, it was this incident that gave rise to the word 'panic' for such a frightened, ill-disciplined withdrawal.

Writing in *The Jewish War* the historian Flavius Josephus records that another unexpected disembodied shout was heard in the Temple at Jerusalem on 15 May AD 70. At the time the city was under siege by Roman troops led by Titus, the son of Emperor Vespasian (ruled AD 69–79). The Jews were brave and defiant, and had been resisting the Romans for over three years, yet the occurrence of several negative omens on the Feast of Unleavened Bread, held on 8 April, had unnerved them. At midday, for example, a mysterious light had shone brightly around the Temple altar and sanctuary; this was followed in the afternoon by the birth of a lamb to a sacrificial cow; and then, at midnight, the East Gate of the Inner Sanctuary had mysteriously opened on its own, whereas it normally required twenty men to move.

But worse forerunners followed. On 15 May, when the Feast of Pentecost was celebrated, the priests who entered the Inner Temple at night to perform the customary ceremonies, first felt a violent movement, such as might be produced by an earthquake, then they heard a loud crash, and afterwards a shout resembling that made by a great multitude, calling out

'Let us leave here!' The Roman stranglehold on the city there-after tightened; it was made worse by a bad outbreak of plague and by starvation, which resulted in the deaths of thousands of Jews, and which led to the final assault and capture of the city on 8 September. All surviving citizens were slaughtered by the Romans, a tragedy which was made worse by the utter destruction of the Temple, the Jewish kingdom's most holy place.

The announcement of a death by a disembodied voice may seem both bizarre and unlikely, although it has happened on several occasions in the more recent past. One of the most interesting examples occurred during the sixteenth century. And strangely, the circumstances of the event have much in common with those attendant upon the death of Pan, notably in that it involved sailors anchored off a small island, although the tars were English, not Greek.

About fifty miles north of the eastern corner of Sicily, in the Tyrrhenian Sea, lies Stromboli, one of the Lipari islands, which is famous for its volcano. The volcanic cone rises to an altitude of 3038 feet, and while it is still active, emitting a steady outpouring of smoke and ash, its eruptions of fire and lava, although of daily occurrence, are mild in intensity. The last major eruption took place there in 1921.

In his book about his travels through the Mediterranean, which he made in 1610, the poet George Sandys (1578–1644) gives a detailed account of the disembodied voice heard by a London merchant named Gresham on the summit of Stromboli. This happened in about 1530 when Gresham was returning from a trading voyage to Palermo, a town on the north shore of Sicily. Shortly after leaving port, Gresham's ship was blown off course by contrary winds. These drove his vessel eastwards, obliging the captain to seek shelter on the lee side of Stromboli, where the ship was anchored until fairer weather prevailed. The delay gave Gresham the opportunity to land on the 5-mile-square volcanic island with eight members of his crew, and at about midday, when the volcano ceased temporar-ily to erupt, they climbed to its summit to examine the crater.

The party made a cautious approach to the smoking aperture, from which the sound of hissing and rumbling came, and which was entirely devoid of other human life, when they all heard, much to their astonishment and terror, a loud voice suddenly cry out, 'Dispatch, dispatch, the rich Antonio is coming!' Believing the voice to be of supernatural origin, Gresham and his men immediately fled the scene and hastily descended the mountain, while behind them the volcano burst into life, sending a sheet of flame into the sky. The party returned, however, to their vessel without harm, and speedily put to sea again, all wondering what the dramatic announcement had meant.

Yet Gresham knew about Antonio, surnamed the Rich, for he was a very wealthy Palermo merchant, who had loaned money to the king of Spain, and to whom his Majesty, in order to secure the loan, had mortgaged two kingdoms. Gresham therefore decided, the winds still proving contrary, to return to Palermo and there make inquiries about him. This was done, and Gresham soon found out, much to his surprise, that not only had the rich Antonio died, but that his death had occurred at about the same time as the words he had heard miraculously spoken on Stromboli's summit.

The incident, hardly surprisingly, had a profound effect on Gresham, not least because it was still generally believed that the craters of volcanoes, along with deep caves and other orifices in the earth, were the routes taken by those souls who went to Hell. This naturally suggested to him that the soul of Antonio was destined for the nether regions. And on his return to London, when granted an audience with Henry VIII, he reported the remarkable incident to the king, who was much interested in it, not least because it was verified under oath by those sailors that had accompanied him on the climbing expedition.

Gresham, moreover, took the voice as a heavenly warning about what might happen to him if he persisted in making money by trade, which now seemed like an activity that led to eternal damnation. He therefore gave up business and distrib-

uted his worldly goods to his kith and kin, keeping only sufficient funds to support himself, and afterwards devoted the
rest of his life to worshipping God.

Shortly after the above incident took place a strange birth
occurred in Assyria, which was attended by several omens, of
which one was vocal. Simon Goulart reports that on 7 March
1532, a woman of that country named Rachienne gave birth to
a son, who not only possessed sparkling eyes and erupted
shining teeth, but was accompanied into the world by a sun
that shone brightly at midnight, while the day itself was dark;
the fall of fire from the sky; a terrible tempest; and the flight
of a dragon across the sky.

And in the midst of them appeared a column or pillar, where there
was a certain writing in Greeke, showing that the end of the world
approached, then was *there a voice heard in the aire, exhorting
every one to prepare himself.* The child having lived two months,
began to speak like one of yeares, & by divers delusions, growes
into such credit, as he was adored and worshipped as a God,
discovering itselfe to be an evill spirit, the which had a great force
of error in all these Countries. [Author's italics]

But despite a birth full of sound and fury, nothing further was
heard about Rachienne's precocious son, which perhaps
means that after 'discovering itselfe to be an evill spirit' he
vanished back into the nether regions.

However, twenty-four years later, in 1556, another voice
was heard in the air, although this time the remarkable event
happened over Germany. Simon Goulart, who is again our
source, records that

In September, over a little Towne in the Marquisate of
Brandenbourg, called *Custerin,* about nine of the clocke at night,
they did see infinite flames of fire comming out of the ayre, and in
the middest two great burning Chevrons. In the ende there was a
voice heard crying, *Miserie, Miserie unto the Church.*

We would probably be right in identifying the 'infinite flames of fire' and the 'two great burning Chevrons' as together forming part of a meteorite fall, although whether the voice that followed it was the sound made by the meteorite as it penetrated the earth's atmosphere, and which happened to resemble spoken words, or if it was an actual disembodied announcement is an open question. Yet as an omen neither the fire nor the sound were very significant. After all, the year 1556–57 was not a particularly bad one for the Catholic Church, which had by then already undergone the damaging attacks of Martin Luther, who died in 1547, and the founding of Protestantism, while the separation of England from the Catholic fold had occurred as early as 1534.

In former ages comets were universally regarded as omens of misfortune, not least because they supposedly forewarned of the downfall or death of emperors and kings. 'When beggars die there are no comets seen,' wrote William Shakespeare. 'The heavens themselves blaze forth the death of princes.' And voices in the air, as we have noted, can have a similar negative meaning. Hence it comes as no surprise to observe that in the years following 1511, when a turret of one of the temples at Tezcuco in Mexico mysteriously caught fire and could not be extinguished, thereby boding ill for the native Aztecs, three comets were also seen above that country, which terrified king Montezuma, for they seemed to promise the return of the white-skinned god Quetzalcoatl and the end of his own dynasty. Then even more ominously in 1519, notes William H. Prescott, 'low voices were heard in the air, and doleful wailings, as if to announce some strange, mysterious calamity!' And behold, not long afterwards Hernando Cortez and his rapacious gang of Spanish thugs arrived, who by a fatal combination of firepower, ruthlessness and treachery overthrew the Aztec empire, robbed it of its gold, and murdered Montezuma. Indeed, never has so much been taken from so many by so few!

One of the most remarkable celestial sounds, which was regarded as, and indeed seemed to be, a favourable omen, is described in the autobiography of the soldier, poet and diplomat Edward, Lord Herbert of Cherbury (1583–1648). Lord Herbert is best known for his singular philosophical work *De Veritate* or 'On Truth', an anti-empirical theory of knowledge, which he completed after much labour at Paris in 1621. Upon having let his Paris host Monsieur Daniel Tieleners read the finished work, Lord Herbert asked the same of the great Dutch scholar and philosopher Hugo Grotius (1583–1645), when he, having escaped from prison in Holland, fled to the French capital. Both men were in fact greatly impressed by Lord Herbert's arguments, and strongly urged him to have the work printed and published. But while gratified by their enthusiastic response, Lord Herbert hesitated to do as they recommended, fearing the opposition and the enmity he would encounter from natural philosophers or scientists. He therefore decided to ask God for a heavenly sign of approval, which he did one fine summer's day at the open south-facing window of his room, his prayer including the words: 'I am not satisfied enough whether I shall publish this book *De Veritate*; if it be for thy glory, I beseech thee give me some sign from heaven; if not, I shall suppress it.' Lord Herbert continues:

I had no sooner spoken these words, but a loud though yet gentle noise came from the heavens, for it was like nothing on earth, which did so comfort and cheer me, that I took my petition as granted, and that I had the sign I demanded, whereupon also I resolved to print my book. This, how strange soever it may seem, I protest before the eternal God is true; neither am I any way superstitiously deceived herein, since I did not only clearly hear the noise, but in the serenest sky that ever I saw, being without all cloud, did to my thinking see the place from whence it came.

De Veritate was in fact published to great acclaim, and it remains as a bulwark against the rising black tide of scientific materialism, which seeks always to rate the evidence of our fallible senses above that of divine revelation.

The voices and sounds mentioned above were all heard entirely by chance, or at least were brought into being without any active participation on the part of the person(s) who heard them, although of course Lord Herbert did pray for a sign. This also applies to most of the disembodied voices described earlier in the book, with the exception of the one heard at the oracular shrine of Trophonius, which only spoke when a suppliant had undergone the necessary preparatory rituals, and also that at Delphi, where the Pythia breathed in mephitic vapours.

Yet the hearing of voices can be encouraged, and in certain cultures, like that of the native North American Indian, such contact with the unseen formed part of a rite of passage into adulthood known as the Guardian Spirit Quest. During this quest all Indian boys and occasionally girls were expected to acquire a spiritual helper or *wyakin*, which often manifested in the guise of a wild creature, such as a bear, a wolf, an elk, or an eagle. The wyakin 'animal' spoke to them and gave them a special name and a song. It also imparted a particular power or skill, which stayed with them throughout lives and which helped to define them as individuals. It was considered so important for a boy to find his guardian spirit, that each male child was told by the village elders: 'Unless you find it when you are a boy, you cannot become much of a man.'

Although the procedure varied from tribe to tribe, what basically happened was this: When the time came for a boy to start his quest, he would first thoroughly cleanse himself by bathing in a river. Then, after offering prayers to the Great Spirit, he went alone and unarmed into the wilderness, taking only a blanket with him for warmth. He walked, sometimes for many miles, to a particular place, which was determined by the type of power he wished to gain. Thus if he wanted bear power, he would camp near to a bear's den; if he wanted eagle power, he would climb to the top of a mountain, and so on. There he stayed and fasted until he either heard a voice or had a vision of 'a strange being, human or animal, that would promise its help in the crises of life'. Sometimes the boy's lonely sojourn lasted for weeks or even months, although if it did the fast would necessarily have to be broken. During the waiting period the boy had to take care of himself, learn to live with solitude, and conquer all his fears. It was in this regard a very challenging experience. The account below, written by an early European missionary in eastern Canada quoted by Diamond Jeness in *The Indians of Canada*, outlines what was heard and seen by a 15-year-old Huron boy during his guardian spirit quest:

After having fasted sixteen days without eating anything, and drinking water only, he suddenly heard this utterance, that came from the sky: 'Take care of this man and let him end his fast.' At the same time, he saw an aged man of rare beauty who came down from the sky, approached him, and, looking kindly at him, said: 'Have courage, I will take care of your life. It is a fortunate thing for you, to have taken me for your master. None of the demons, who haunt these countries, shall have any power to harm you. One day you will see your hair as white as mine. You will have four children; the first two and the last will be males and the third will be a girl; after that, your wife will hold the relation of sister to you.'

And the wyakin's predictions all came true! Furthermore, the boys who found their guardian spirit also discovered that it led to an improvement in their appearance: they became handsomer, taller and stronger, and they walked and spoke with a more confident and manly demeanour. A Nez Percé Indian named Yellow Wolf failed his first guardian spirit quest. The second took place the following year, when he was 13 years old. His tribe live in the foothills of the Rocky Mountains, and on the second occasion he was sent to their wildest part.

After many suns without food, I slept and had something like a dream. You white people call it a trance. A figure stood in front of me and talked to me. 'My boy, look at me. Take a good look at me! If you do what I tell you to do, you will be as I am. I will give you power. You may think I am nothing. You may think that I am only bones, but I am alive. You can see me now. I am Hemene Moxmox.'

It was the spirit of a wolf that was talking to me. Its colour was a sort of yellow, and it seemed to float in the air. It talked to me like a human being, and it gave me its power. . . . That is how I got the name Yellow Wolf.

The wyakin, which resembles in many ways the Greek daimonion, could save a brave's life in a crisis. Here, for example, is what happened to Yellow Wolf a few years later, when he was guarding some horses on a freezing night:

Riding horseback, I was doubled over and my eyes were closed because of the cold wind. I went sound asleep. I did not know anything and I must have been near death, when I felt something tightly touch my thigh and shake it. Then I heard a voice speaking – 'What are you doing? Wake up! You are dead! Go home!'

A far more recent and somewhat perplexing example of an odd sound was reported to me by a Leeds University student named Christophe Marshall. It happened one evening in August 1999, when Christophe was alone in his flat. At the time he was sitting in an armchair and watching television, with the room light, which had a dimmer switch, turned down low.

Suddenly I heard someone breathing very heavily in my right ear. At first I thought it was the television and passed it off as being like when you hear a phone on the TV and think it is your own phone. It went momentarily and I continued to watch. Then it happened again, very loud in my right ear. It was distracting, almost to the point of annoyance. I pressed the mute sound on the remote control and sat for a moment. It happened again, four to five breaths in my right ear.

Shocked and frightened, Christophe jumped up and turned all the lights full on, trying desperately to understand what had caused the sound. The flat had no heating pipes or vents that might have been responsible, and a search revealed that there was no one there who had entered unannounced and played a trick on him. Indeed, all the outside doors and windows were locked against intruders. Christophe's failure to work out how the breathing sound had happened left him very puzzled. 'I have to admit that to this day I do not know what caused the breathing,' he said, adding, 'It was definite breathing and was right next to my ear.'

Aside from the rather unlikely possibility that the noise was caused by some temporary physical change in Christophe's right ear, perhaps involving earwax, it seems that he did hear a disembodied breathing which perhaps originated from an unseen presence hovering near to him. But if so, it is difficult to understand why the presence should only have breathed into his ear and not spoken. Christophe had never heard such an inexplicable breathing sound before, and has not done so since.

A somewhat similar anomalous sound was heard in the early nineteenth century by a French doctor named Leuret, although he regarded it as an hallucination. The strange experience happened to Dr Leuret when, having gone down with influenza, he was put to bed and bled with leeches. The loss of blood, however, so weakened him that he remained only semi-conscious for the next eight hours. One of his attendants then came to his bedside to assist him, and Dr Leuret heard him, or so he thought, place a bottle on the marble top of the table beside his bed. 'And soon afterwards,' Dr Leuret adds, 'a crepitating sound, like that which arises from the action of strong acid on a piece of carbonate of lime. I thought that some acid had been spilt on the marble table, and I admonished the persons in attendance of their carelessness. At first they thought I was dreaming, then, that I was delirious; they next endeavoured to undeceive me, and assured me that there was no bottle on the table, nor had any acid been spilt.' (Edmund Parish, *Hallucinations and Illusions*)

Hence the sound was so real and seemingly external to

121

himself, that Dr Leuret was at first convinced that what he had heard had actually happened. Yet no bottle had in fact been placed on the table, nor had any acid been spilled on it. This led Dr Leuret, who worked with patients suffering from hallucinations, to assume that he had himself been the victim of a similar misapprehension. Yet we cannot necessarily agree with him, for as all the previously discussed cases have shown, sounds can manifest in space quite apart from the material causes of them, whether these be a loved one's throat, a musical instrument, the clashing of weapons, or a bottle and some spilt acid.

An equally strange sound event, although one that involved a voice, happened about six years ago to London resident David Hunter, a 54-year-old former policeman and radio ham, when he was sitting at his office desk. He was, he told me, in a stable and upbeat frame of mind at the time, and he had no particular worries or concerns, other than those relating to his usual daily chores. But suddenly he heard within his own head:

a totally unrecognized seemingly male 'voice' that shocked me with the imperative, 'all systems go' sort of clarity. If you have ever listened to a crystal set, it was that sort of plugged-in sound, clear of the external 'colourations' one gets from sinus, cheekbones, earwax! The interesting bit is that 'the message' was spoken very fast, so fast I couldn't make it out, maybe five or six words (a sentence perhaps) and I knew it was important, and I knew it had been planted in my subconscious, if you like. But I knew I would not remember it in my conscious state. It's the only experience that I have had in 54 years, and I'm still waiting for the revelation! It was definitely NOT airborne acoustics.

David was completely unable to account for this very odd happening, despite being familiar with radio waves and with the fact that 'the human cranium is resonant on several of these (microwave) frequencies in the 700 and 1300 MHz ranges'. He also noted: 'It was a startling experience to "hear"

122

such an obviously internalized voice, which had the impact. It was not *of* me but *inside* my head. It also seemed to have such clarity, as a digitized or synthesized source, urgent, and imperative.' And while like many middle-aged people David remembers the story, which reputedly happened in the early 1960s, of the man who picked up a BBC long wave broadcast on his false teeth, he does not think that a similar anomalous reception was responsible for his one-off experience! So he may possibly have heard part of an unsuccessful attempt by his daimonion to get a message through to him, but which for some reason it could neither complete nor render understandable.

I have mentioned some other examples of disembodied voices whose words have not only been unclear but which have had an odd quality. One example from the last chapter was the music heard by a dying women and her companion, which sounded 'like voices singing, she said, but the words were indistinguishable, and the whole thing struck her as "strange, different, on another wavelength".' Another appears in the Munich Collection, also included in *Hallucinations and Illusions* by Edmund Parish, which quotes a 37-year-old serviceman, who, when sitting at his writing-table one day, said he 'seemed to hear a voice calling out some words to me. . . . When I tried to think whose the voice resembled, I found that it sounded distinctly like my grandmother (on my mother's side). The words that she had uttered chimed in with my thoughts, and that was what had so surprised me when I heard them.'

Music without a visible source has been frequently reported in the past, often as an accompaniment to someone's death, although its occurrence is now apparently less common, presumably because there are so many everyday sources of music in the form of radios, record players, CD players, musak and the like, that those hearing it tend to ascribe its manifestation to one or other of these.

The god Pan, for example, in addition to alarming travellers by shouting loudly, was believed to play a reed pipe and to charm those who were fortunate enough to hear him with his divine melodies. Or as Lucretius puts it: 'Music far-heard by the country-folk when Pan, tossing the pine-branches that wreathe his brutish head, runs his arched lips again and again along the wind-mouthed reeds, so that the pipe's wildwood rhapsody flows on unbroken.' And the satyrs or fauns, which were also goat-legged and cloven-footed country deities, were thought to play both the Pan pipe and the lyre, and to similarly surprise and enchant the passing traveller with them.

But in case the reader thinks that if ethereal music was (and sometimes still is) heard in country places, it did or does not originate from either Pan or the satyrs, the following twentieth-century description of an encounter with a music-making youthful 'Pan' might prove salutary. The witnesses were Professor Charles Seltman and four companions, who in 1930 were driving together along a pot-holed country road towards Corinth, in Greece. There was a sandstone bank beside the road, topped by a low hedge, beyond which was a vineyard.

Behind this hedge and among the vines HE showed himself. He was a Hellenistic, little-boy Pan. Had he been human one would have said a little seven-year-old. Black rough hair, very pointed ears, a snub nose and a body beautifully shaped, and coloured by the sun to a deep chocolate cream. He was naked to the waist. . . . In one hand he held a small curved piece of stick; in the other a little syrinx, or 'Pan pipes', on which he blew a tinny tune. Had he the legs of a little goat? We never knew. But he cried out to us in a voice high-pitched but of astonishing strength . . . 'Dance all of you, dance; I am making music for you.'

Another instance of playerless music being heard happened during the youth of St Dunstan, a tenth-century monk. Dunstan, who was of aristocratic birth, was brought as a child into the household of King Athelstan (*c.* 895–940) to be the playmate of Athelstan's much younger brother Edmund (*c.* 922–946). But one morning in AD 941, when Dunstan was 16 years old, he was called into the chamber of lady Ethelwyn and her maidens to help them choose some patterns for the vestments they were embroidering. The women were clustered together beneath one of the chamber's narrow windows, and as Dunstan went over to them, a soft, low, delightful music suddenly erupted from the end of the room. Astonished, the Queen and her women stopped what they were doing, and then, crying out to Dunstan that he knew more than a good Christian ought, rushed out of the room in alarm. The incident, which was as much a surprise to Dunstan as it was to the ladies, led to the young man having to undergo a test to show he was not a witch, and when he was found not guilty, he took refuge with Bishop Elfege at Winchester, who persuaded him to become a monk. Thus the mysterious music was directly responsible for Dunstan entering the church and to becoming in due course a saint. He later reputedly grasped the Devil by the nose with red-hot pincers!

Several interesting accounts of music with no visible source are reported from eastern Canada by folklorist Dr Helen Creighton. For example, a resident of Parker's Cove, Nova Scotia, said that on the March evening when her brother died, her sister who was at his bedside with him, heard a choir of voices sing an entire rendition of the song 'A Perfect Day', which seemingly came from a corner of the room. And that happened, she noted, before the days of the wireless. Similarly, on the day that the daughter of a family was dying at their farmhouse at Middleton, Nova Scotia, several passersby heard the sounds of beautiful music coming from the house, although in reality none was being made there. And when a man at Ship Harbour was dying, both he and his wife clearly heard a violin being played. 'I didn't recognize any particular tune,' she said; 'just the sound of music and nobody anywhere near to be making it.'

We are given a poetic impression of such music by Edward Young in his *The Complaint: or, Night-Thoughts on Life, Death, and Immortality* (1742–45):

High Heavn's *Orchestra* chaunts *Amen* to Man.
Hear I, or dream I hear, their distant Strain,
Sweet to the Soul, and tasting strong of Heav'n,
Soft-wafted on celestial *Pity's* Plume,
Thro' the vast Spaces of the Universe,
To chear me in this melancholy Gloom?

Another strange case of disembodied voices being heard, which happened in about 1991, was reported to me by Carl Magedera, although its occurrence in a cemetery makes it perhaps less surprising than it might otherwise have been. On the spring morning in question, which was 'clear and bright, without there being much heat', 15-year-old Carl and his father took a walk through North Watford Cemetery, off North Western Avenue. Then Carl was suddenly stunned to hear voices nearby greeting one another, although there was absolutely nobody in sight. He remembers that one belonged to a man, who was speaking to a child 'in a fashion that a well-educated Victorian might greet a young street boy. The voices sounded very cheerful, and one commented on the fine weather.' Yet despite Carl clearly hearing the mysterious voices, he says that his father has no recollection of them. This perhaps means that instead of being ghostly, the voices came from an earlier age, which was presumably caused by a 'crack' momentarily appearing in the fabric of space/time, thereby enabling Carl, but not his father, to catch some greetings that were exchanged there long ago. Carl had never, he tells me, heard a disembodied voice before, and neither has he heard one since. This likewise indicates that the occurrence was a one-off accident without purpose or meaning.

The reports of the noises made by invisible or non-existent armies find a modern parallel in the strange case involving the ocean liner *Queen Mary*, which during the Second World War, while attempting to evade German U-boats, collided with and sank a cruiser escort named HMS *Curaçao*, an accident that cost the lives of some 300 sailors aboard the smaller vessel.

Some 40 years later, after the *Queen Mary* had been retired from service and sold to the Americans as a tourist attraction at Long Beach, California, a carpenter named John Smith was one day working below decks in the bow section, when he suddenly heard, coming as if from nowhere, the sound of frightened cries and voices, and also that of rushing water. When he scrambled back up on deck, he was surprised to discover that nothing had taken place outside to account for the sounds, and he certainly had no knowledge of the dreadful accident involving the ship many years before. Moreover, in 1981, when an American psychic researcher named William G. Roll spent time in the bow section investigating the incident, he also heard similar voices, whose source he likewise failed to locate. That night he left a sound-activated tape recorder below decks, and incredibly, when he listened to the tape next day, he discovered that it had picked up the same sounds, which certainly proved that neither he nor John Smith had been mistaken about what they had heard.

Together, the two incidents suggest that the numerous and mysterious disembodied voices heard may have originated from the day of the accident, and were somehow impressed on the ether by the anxiety and alarm experienced by those aboard both vessels at the time.

Finally, it is pertinent to confute one of the most memorable cinematographic instances of a disembodied voice, which is portrayed in the film biography of Harry Houdini, the famous American magician and escapologist. According to the film, this remarkable incident supposedly happens after the handcuffed Houdini jumps through a hole into the ice-covered Detroit River, which is a publicity stunt intended to excite interest in his show at a local theatre. Houdini successfully extricates himself from the handcuffs, but on rising to the surface, he finds that he cannot locate the exit hole in the ice. But then, when he is in danger of drowning, he is dramatically saved by hearing his mother's voice calling to him, for by swimming towards the sound, he is brought to the hole.

What actually happened was rather different. Houdini did

in fact jump handcuffed through a hole cut in the ice covering the frozen Detroit River one morning early in the winter of 1906. He sank to the bottom, where he soon freed himself from the handcuffs, but the river current proved stronger than he had expected and it carried him downstream away from the exit hole as he surfaced. He came up to find ice above him, but thankfully he discovered, as portrayed in the film, that 'between the surface of the water and the undersurface of the ice was a little air space, about half an inch wide. By lying on my back and poking my nose into this gently, I could fill my lungs'. (Harold Kellock, *Houdini*, [1928])

Houdini knew that he only needed to inhale some water with the air to start choking, which would have caused him to drown. Yet he managed to stay calm. Each time he took in a little air and then swam about to see if he could find the exit hole, before stopping to breathe again. However, while this was going on, those waiting for him on the ice were becoming increasingly worried about his safety, especially after nearly eight minutes had gone by. But nevertheless, it was not his mother's voice that directed him to the exit hole, but rather the splash made by a rope that was thrown through it into the river by his assistant. 'After what seemed about an hour,' recalled Houdini, 'I saw the rope flash into the water, not very far away, and you bet I made for it. That was that.' He was doubly lucky in that had he remained any longer in the cold river, he would have lost all bodily sensation along with the power of muscular movement, which would certainly have caused him to drown.

7   The Deity Speaks

Fear came upon me, and trembling, which made all my bones shake. Then a spirit passed before my face; the hair of my flesh stood up: It stood still, but I could not discern the form thereof; an image *was* before mine eyes, *there was* silence, and I heard a voice, *saying*, Shall mortal man be more just than God?

From *The Book of Job*, Chapter IV

Although in the previous pages I have mentioned the shouts reputedly made by Pan and the voice of Apollo, little has otherwise been said about the deity that speaks. Such an event, however, has happened frequently in the past, and it is still on occasions reported today. Yet I have pointed out that whereas people often hear an unrecognized external disembodied voice, which may offer them advice or impart a warning or a prophecy, it is comparatively rare for them to consider it to be the voice of God. For when God does speak, or at least when He is thought to speak, it is either the quality of His voice, or what is said, or the associated events that occur, which together distinguish His voice from that of a daimonion or from some other source.

In the ancient world it was universally believed that the gods directly communicated with mankind, which could happen in a number of different ways. Natural phenomena like thunder, lightning, hurricanes, hailstones, meteorites and comets, for example, were all regarded as expressions of the sky god's will. These occurrences were not only frightening but often actually harmful, and so indicated annoyance or even anger on the part of the god. Moreover, thunder was regarded in early times as the real voice of the sky god, which could be directly understood by those gifted with sufficient insight. We find this belief current as late as AD 33, for when Jesus rode into Jerusalem on an ass, St John records that, 'Then came there a voice from heaven, *saying*, I have both glorified *it*, and will glorify *it* again. The people therefore, that stood by, and heard *it*, said that it thundered: others said, An angel spake to him' (*John*, XII, 28–9). Another similar meteorological source of Jehovah's voice is given in *Job* XXXVIII,1, which says that 'the Lord answered Job out of the whirlwind'.

A more personal form of communication was believed to occur in dreams, which were said to be sent directly by a god or by God. Everyone from the king down paid attention to their dreams, and those which were in any way odd or unusual would be related to diviners, so that their meaning could be revealed. Birds – particularly birds of prey, like eagles - were also thought to be divine messengers, and the interpretation of what their aerial activities meant was a job left to specially trained experts, the augurs. The will of the gods was also and more bizarrely revealed by the shape and the position of the internal organs of sacrificed animals (a method of divination known as haruspicy), by the way in which chickens ate, by the first words heard spoken on entering or leaving a particular place, and a host of other methods of fortune-telling, some of which, like casting the runes, palmistry and astrology, are still with us today.

Such methods of prediction all had the disadvantage of requiring interpreters, whose skill or degree of insight varied. Indeed, being a seer was a hazardous job for anyone who presumed to advise the king or some other powerful figure about what the gods intended doing, but who gave wrong or unwanted answers. A very narrow escape from premature death was experienced by the Graeco-Roman astrologer Thrasyllus, who had disillusioned the young Tiberius with his unfulfilled prophecies of high office and coming greatness for him, and who was about to be pushed over a cliff on the island of Rhodes, when he suddenly pointed to a ship on the horizon and told Tiberius that it brought good news. And fortunately for Thrasyllus, the vessel did in fact carry a letter recalling Tiberius to Rome. Soon after Tiberius arrived back in the capital, he was adopted by the Emperor Augustus, whom he succeeded when he died.

But clearly, the interpretation of dreams and omens, even if we assume they are divine messages, was (and is) always open to error, which made them something of a mixed blessing. A disembodied voice, however, could not only be understood by everyone, but its manifestation was sufficiently unusual and wonderful to suggest that it was uttered by a god, particularly when it spoke within the confines of a temple or other holy place. Nevertheless, the words of the deity were not always entirely straightforward, which is why Apollo, for example, who was believed to speak through the Pythia at Delphi, was surnamed *Loxias*, meaning 'the Ambiguous'.

The god worshipped by the Jews of the Old Testament was the most vocal of the ancient deities. His power was also thought to manifest through His voice, for it was by uttering commands that He supposedly created, from primordial darkness and chaos, the earth and all that is in it in six days. 'And God said, Let there be light: and there was light,' is the first recorded divine instruction in *Genesis* (I, 3). Such voice-induced creativity continued on each succeeding day. On the fifth day, for example, God ordered: 'Let the earth bring forth the living creature after his kind, cattle, and creeping thing, and the beast of the earth after his kind: and it was so.' Man was similarly brought into existence on the sixth day.

However, the creation of human beings, as portrayed in *Genesis*, is somewhat confusing, owing to the fact that there are two separate accounts therein, one designated Yahwist, the other Priestly, although most people are familiar with God's generation of Adam, the first man, 'in his own image', who is afterwards transferred to the delightful garden of Eden. There

131

God speaks to Adam as a disembodied voice, warning him that, 'Of every tree of the garden thou mayest freely eat: But of the tree of the knowledge of good and evil, thou shalt not eat of it: for in the day that thou eatest thereof thou shalt surely die.' It is both interesting and relevant to note that God's first words to Adam take the form of this short warning, wherein they are similar to those cautions given by disembodied voices throughout history.

According to the Yahwist version of the creation myth, God then made Eve, the first woman, from one of Adam's ribs. Eve, however, is soon persuaded by the serpent to eat a fruit from the forbidden tree, and she afterwards prompts Adam to do the same, whereupon they both become aware of their nakedness and of their sexuality. When they later hide in shame from the sight of God, their disobedience is revealed. Eve is accordingly punished by being made to conceive and bear children, and both she and Adam, upon being clothed in skins, are expelled from Eden.

God afterwards speaks to their sons Cain and Abel, and then, about 1426 years later, to Noah, the descendant of Seth, Adam and Eve's third son, whom he tells to build a giant boat or Ark, and thereby to save his family and representative pairs of animals from the coming Flood. Next, after another very long interval, God converses with 90-year-old Abraham, whom he orders to be circumcised. God also advises Sarah, Abraham's post-menopausal wife, that she will bear a child. With the birth of her infant, who is named Isaac, the mythological origins of the Jewish nation are effectively brought to an end.

Such vocal exchanges between God and the aforementioned individuals, while apocryphal in nature, are characteristic of what happens in myths from around the world. Thus a god commands, and his hearers obey – or they are punished if they do not. And later, when the historical period is reached, the deity concerned selects a particular individual, to whom he verbally imparts various laws governing how that person and his tribe shall live. If they subsequently disobey the God-given laws, they are severely punished. Thus the civilizing laws are divine, and disobedience to them is both wrong and sacrilegious.

The chosen recipient for the bulk of Jewish law was Moses. The Jews were in captivity in Egypt when God first spoke to him, and the initial contact was made at Midian, where the young Moses, having killed an Egyptian (in about 1491 BC), is forced to flee and where he becomes a shepherd. One day Moses, upon driving his flock to the mountain at Horeb, comes across a burning bush that strangely was not consumed by the flames. Then, to Moses's astonishment, God calls to him from out of the bush, saying, 'Moses, Moses.' He nervously replies, 'Here *am* I.' God next tells Moses that He intends helping him to free his people from Egypt, and that he must then lead them across the Sinai desert to the promised land in Canaan. Soon afterwards, in His most intimate communication, God informs Moses that His name is Jehovah, which He did not reveal to Abraham, to Isaac, or to Jacob. And from this time on Jehovah often speaks to Moses.

When the Jews finally escape from Egypt, Moses as instructed conducts them through the Sinai peninsula towards Canaan. After a journey of three months they arrive at, and camp beside, the mountain at Sinai. Almost immediately, Moses is summoned by Jehovah to the top of the mountain, which lies hidden within a thick layer of cloud. Speaking from within the cloud, Jehovah tells him, 'Now therefore, if ye will obey my voice indeed, and keep my covenant, then ye shall be a peculiar treasure unto me above all people: for all the earth *is* mine. And ye shall be unto me a kingdom of priests, and an holy nation.' Moses is then told to descend the mountain and tell his people what has been said, and later, he is ordered to return to the summit on the third day.

What happens on the third day is significant in view of what was said earlier about thunder, for *Exodus* records that, 'And it came to pass on the third day in the morning, that there were thunders and lightnings, and a thick cloud upon the mount, and the voice of the trumpet exceeding loud; so that all the people that *was* in the camp trembled.' It is particularly noteworthy that the 'voice of the trumpet exceeding loud' resembles the trumpets sounding in the air referred to in the previous chapter.

Moses takes his people part of the way up the mountain with him, but on reaching the boundary beyond which they are forbidden to go, he leaves them there and proceeds alone to the summit. Then within the black cloud that still covers it, Jehovah gives Moses the all-important Ten Commandments, which still form the basis of Western morality. And while that divine communication is taking place, it is further recorded in *Exodus*: 'And all the people saw the thunderings, and the lightnings, and the noise of the trumpet, and the mountain smoking: and when the people saw *it*, they removed, and stood afar off.' This circumstance very much resembles what happened when Jesus rode into Jerusalem on an ass, for then 'the people ... said that it thundered: others said, an angel spoke to him,' which may mean that Moses did not actually hear Jehovah's voice then, but rather intuitively interpreted thunder as divine commands. This is also suggested by the fact that when Moses descends the mountain to give the Ten Commandments to his followers, they say to him, perhaps remembering the lightning which accompanied their recitation: 'Let not God speak to us, lest we die.'

When Moses returns into the thick darkness, he is again addressed by Jehovah, who first tells him, 'Thus thou shalt say unto the children of Israel, Ye have seen that I have talked with you from heaven.' Such an observation, however, could only have been made by those watching if they had heard thunder and seen flashes of lightning. Jehovah then imparts to Moses a long, mixed bag of additional laws and judgements, which include how masters should treat servants, the care of widows and orphans, the penalties for various offences, how a physical injury must generally be punished by inflicting the same wound on the perpetrator – the text reads, 'Life for life, eye for eye, tooth for tooth, hand for hand, foot for foot, burning for burning, wound for wound, stripe for stripe' –

that witchcraft and having sex with animals are offences punishable by death, that no other gods must be worshipped, and so on.

Nevertheless, it is as well to remember that when, some 500 years later, the prophet Elijah goes to the sacred mountain at Horeb and lives there in a cave for forty days and nights, he is also spoken to by Jehovah. But the text makes it clear that His voice is not a product of the elements, saying: 'And a great and strong wind rent the mountains, and brake in pieces the rocks before the Lord; *but* the Lord was not in the wind: and after the wind an earthquake; *but* the Lord *was* not in the earthquake: And after the earthquake a fire; *but* the Lord *was* not in the fire: and after the fire a still small voice. And it was *so*, when Elijah heard *it*, that he wrapped his face in his mantle, and went out, and stood in the entering in of the cave. And behold, *there came* a voice unto him, and said, What doest thou here, Elijah?' (*1 Kings*, XIX, 11–13)

Furthermore, on the morning following the reportage of the above-mentioned laws to those waiting for him Moses returned to the mountain accompanied by Aaron, Nadab, Abihu and seventy elders, who all 'saw the God of Israel: and *there was* under his feet as it were a paved work of a sapphire stone, and as it were the body of heaven in *his* clearness.' This mass viewing of God suggests that He was actually there on the mountain, which gives credence to the reality of His voice. Nevertheless, Moses thereafter proceeds by himself to the summit, which is still covered with cloud. He stays there for many days, but on the seventh day Jehovah at last calls to him from out of the cloud, whereupon 'the sight of the glory of the Lord was like a devouring fire on the top of the mount in the eyes of the children of Israel'. This suggests that Jehovah's voice arose in some way from out of what appears to have been a sudden fiery, possibly volcanic, upsurge. And oddly, Moses remains atop the mountain for thirty-three more days, making a total of forty days. During this period Moses is given lengthy, exact instructions about how to make a tabernacle, which is to be built when he returns to the base camp.

The tabernacle, a specially consecrated, elaborate tent, was in due course constructed far from the Sinai base camp, and when Moses entered it, 'the cloudy pillar descended, and stood at the door of the tabernacle, and *the* Lord talked with Moses. . . . And the Lord spoke unto Moses face to face, as a man speaketh to his friend.' This of course suggests that speech came out of the cloud and that Jehovah spoke directly to Moses, although we regretfully have only his word for it, as no one else was allowed anywhere near the tabernacle.

It is from within the cloudy pillar that Jehovah really comes into His own where law making is concerned, and the remainder of *Exodus* as well as the following books of *Leviticus*, *Numbers* and *Deuteronomy* are replete with His dictated laws, which cover every facet of Jewish communal life in those far-off days. Jehovah in fact had difficulty in keeping quiet, which must have greatly tested the mnemonic skills of Moses, as well as trying the patience of the scribes who were afterwards obliged to write it all down. We can only be grateful that it happened then, and not now!

But such verbal instruction by Jehovah, the 'God of Israel', was by no means limited to Him. Individuals belonging to other ancient tribes and races, who were polytheistic, also claimed to have been instructed by one or other of their gods. Indeed, the best known example of such divine law-giving happened centuries before Jehovah spoke to Moses, at about the same time in fact that the Jewish patriarch Abraham and his family were residing at Ur, in Mesopotamia. The man who claimed to have been spoken to by a god was Hammurabi, who reigned at Babylon for forty-three years, from 1792 to 1750 BC. Hammurabi was king of the Amorites, a Semitic people who spoke Akkadian, and who, having inherited a small kingdom from his father Sin-muballit, went on to expand his domain throughout his long reign, until at his death it included all of Mesopotamia and stretched as far west as the Mediterranean. But despite Hammurabi being the greatest ruler of the time, who unified the many kingdoms of the Middle East into one great empire, little was known about him for many years. This was mainly because his kingdom suffered an eclipse at his death, due to the fact that neither his son nor his grandson were respectively able to resist the internal challenges or the external threats to their realm.

Then in 1901, some French archaeologists working under J. de Morgan at Susa, dug up a number of large black diorite (or greenstone) fragments, which, when they fitted them together, produced an eight-foot tall, roughly lozenge-shaped pillar or stele. Both sides of the stele bore horizontal columns of cuneiform writing, one of which also included a striking intaglio representation of a meeting between King Hammurabi and the sun-god Shamash. When translated, the cuneiform script was revealed as beginning with a biography of Hammurabi, describing his greatness and his conquests, which was followed by a unique list of 282 laws and commands, known now as the Code of Hammurabi, which had evidently been directly imparted to the king by Shamash, and which, in both their number and content, are remarkably similar to those later given to Moses by Jehovah. Indeed, if we can accept that Jehovah actually spoke to Moses and gave him the Ten Commandments and the other laws recorded in the Old Testament, then it is equally probable that Shamash (or at least a divine voice) was similarly helpful to Hammurabi some 300 years earlier.

But although the stele was found in pieces at Susa, a city of the Elamite kingdom, it had originally been erected by King Hammurabi at Sippar, a city on the Euphrates. It was apparently removed from Sippar after Hammurabi's death by an Elamite conqueror, who transported it to Susa as part of his spoil.

At Sippar, the tablet had stood in Shamash's temple, where it could be consulted by anyone who wished to know the law of the land, while at the same time declaiming the sun-god's part in the operation. The latter was of particular relevance to the citizens of Sippar, because Shamash was the tutelary god of their city: hence the laws inscribed on the tablet were given to them by their own deity. But the code was more than just a list of laws: it was also a social and moral guide, describing how citizens were supposed to treat one another and their servants and animals. It also pointedly reminded everyone that social misbehaviour and law-breaking were sinful, and would bring down upon them, either in this life or the next, the wrath of all-seeing Shamash.

The punishments prescribed for law-breakers are uniformly harsh by today's liberal 'the criminal is also a victim' standards, for they are based on the straightforward principle of 'eye for eye, tooth for tooth', although in some cases the punishment clearly exceeds the crime. Thus the code says, for example, that if a man strikes his father, his hands shall be cut off. The punishments also vary depending upon the social status of the parties. Hence if someone blinds an equal's eye, or crushes his limb, or knocks out his tooth, then he shall be blinded in the same eye, crushed in the same leg, and have the same tooth knocked out. Yet if the victim is a poor man, then a payment of one mina of silver is sufficient recompense. And if the victim is the slave of a free man, the defendant has to pay half the slave's price, although whether the money went to the slave or to his owner is unclear.

In the carving of Hammurabi and Shamash, the monarch is represented as standing before the seated god, who delivers his laws and judgements to Hammurabi by word of mouth. The throne on which Shamash sits forms part of a raised brick dais, the two together suggesting that the encounter between king and god took place at the top of either a mountain or, as seems more likely, *ziqqurat* or pyramidal stage tower. The word *ziqqurat* means 'Mountain of God'. By tradition, the summits of mountains and of raised places generally were considered dwelling places of gods, for as the Psalmist says, 'I cried unto the Lord with my voice, and he heard me out of his holy hill.' All Mesopotamian cities, which were built on the low-lying, mountainless river plain, included a tall, brick-built ziqqurat – that of Ur had a height of 70 feet – dedicated to the city's deity, at whose apex was a chamber wherein the god (or goddess) might descend and take his rest whenever it was convenient to him. The ziqqurat of Babylon was the infamous tower of Babel, whose 'top may reach unto heaven'.

We can therefore imagine Hammurabi climbing to the summit of the ziqqurat at Sippar, much as Moses later ascended to the top of Mount Sinai, and where he may have stayed, as did Moses, for several, if not many, days. He was there spoken to by a mysterious voice, which intoned the laws that were later inscribed on the diorite stele. It is not necessary to believe that Hammurabi actually saw the god, although their 'meeting' was portrayed as a face-to-face encounter by the artist who carved the scene. And while archaeologists tend to dismiss the event as wholly symbolic, we may reasonably argue that a disembodied voice probably did speak to Hammurabi, that it gave the essence if not the entirety of the laws written on the stele, and that it was believed by Hammurabi to come from Shamash, the sun-god.

Interestingly, Hammurabi is mentioned in *Genesis* XIV, 1 under the name of Amraphel, king of Shinar, who joined forces with Arioch, king of Ellasar, Chedorlaomer, king of Elam, and Tidal, king of nations, to attack the cities of Sodom and Gomorrah, and which therefore places the operation too early (*c.* 1792–87) in Hammurabi's reign, before he attacked and overthrew the monarchs with whom he had then fought.

As far as can be determined, Abraham left Ur with his wife Sarah, father Terah, and nephew Lot, two or three years before that war. He was then 75 years old, and he would have been wholly familiar with the established and traditional laws of the land, which in many ways were just as rigorous as those making up the Code of Hammurabi. This perhaps means that Abraham introduced the Mesopotamian concept of climbing a holy mountain to meet with God and thereby to receive his commandments to his fellow Jews. But what is extraordinary is that the above-mentioned description of God in *Exodus*, which includes the sentence 'there were under his feet as it were a paved work of a sapphire stone', could equally well be referring to the brickwork shown under Shamash's feet in the carving on Hammurabi's stele.

What is likewise remarkable is the fact that during this same early period, that is, between about 1800 and 1550 BC, there came into full flower the Minoan civilization of Crete, known to archaeologists as the Middle Minoan Period, which is named after Minos, the island's most famous king. His vast, many-roomed palace at Knossos, which was excavated by Sir Arthur Evans, probably gave rise to the story of the Labyrinth and its bull-headed inhabitant, the Minotaur. Greek myth records that Minos and his brothers Sarpedon and Rhadamanthus were the sons of Zeus, the sky god, and the beautiful mortal Europa, although some say that the Minos who built Knossos was the grandson of this Minos. Zeus in fact had a very close connection with Crete, for it was held that after he was born, in order to prevent him being eaten by his father Cronus, he was carried by Mother Earth to Crete and hidden there in a cave named Dicte on the Aegean Hill, near Lyctos. Later, when he grew to manhood, he removed himself to Mount Ida, where he briefly lived in another cave and consorted with the shepherds who grazed their flocks on Ida's grassy slopes.

Following the birth of her triplets, Europa took them with her to Crete, where she married King Asterius, who in due course, their marriage proving childless, adopted them and made them his heirs. The sons each inherited one third of the island on Asterius's death, although a homosexual love affair later caused Sarpedon to leave Crete and migrate to Caria in Asia Minor, where he founded the city of Miletus, named after his youthful lover.

Minos, however, set to work building the city of Knossos and in trying to civilize his rude and uncultivated subjects. In this he was aided by Rhadamanthus, whose love of justice prompted him to obtain the requisite laws directly from his father Zeus. He did this by taking himself off to Zeus's former grotto on the Aegean Hill, in whose dark and holy depths he prayed, and was spoken to by his father, who gave him the laws in question. Tradition also says that Rhadamanthus was imparted new and updated laws by Zeus when he visited the

Dictaean cave nine years later, but afterwards he was obliged to flee Crete, having accidentally killed a relative, although his place in the sacred cave was taken by Minos. Indeed, Minos has been called the Cretan Moses, although this title really belongs to Rhadamanthus. The Dictaean oracle, for so we may call it, was therefore very similar to that of Trophonius. After their deaths, Minos and Rhadamanthus, along with Aeacus, son of Zeus and Aegina, were said to have become the judges of the dead.

Another divine dispensation of laws occurred among the Etruscans, who emigrated to Italy from Lydia in the eighth century BC, although because Tages, the deity concerned, actually appeared to some of them, we cannot legitimately include such directly-given declamations in this narrative. The Tagetic doctrine, for so the laws are together called, was hurriedly inscribed on wax tablets by the incredulous listeners, to whom Tages also brought the art of haruspicy or liver-reading. The interested reader will find this remarkable event fully described in my earlier book entitled *Supernatural Disappearances*.

One of the most famous law-makers of the ancient world was Lycurgus of Sparta, who was so upstanding and wise that, like Socrates some 450 years later, he was praised by Apollo when the god spoke to him through the Pythia at Delphi. The Lord of Light addressed him by saying, 'Beloved of the gods, and rather a god than a man', and it was from Apollo that Lycurgus claimed to have received the laws from which the citizens of Sparta benefited.

Lycurgus, the second son of Eunomos, king of Sparta, was born in about 926 BC. He was therefore a contemporary of the Jewish prophet Elijah the Tishbite, who was also spoken to by Jehovah. Sparta was already unusual for having two kings, a custom which had begun in 1102 BC, when Argia, the wife of King Aristodemus, bore twin sons, named Procles and Eurysthenes, but refused to say which of them had been born first. They were therefore made joint kings, a custom which was continued by their descendants.

When Eunomos, a great-great-grandson of Procles, was stabbed to death in 907 BC, his crown passed to Polydectes, his eldest son and Lycurgus's half-brother. The other king was Archelaus. However, Polydectes died not long afterwards, but just as Lycurgus was about to assume the throne in his stead, it was discovered that Polydectes's wife was pregnant. Lycurgus therefore waited to see if she would bear a son, and when she gave birth to a boy, who was named Charilaus, he became the child's guardian and the *de facto* co-ruler. However, Polydectes's widow, in an attempt to remain queen, not only tried to persuade Lycurgus to marry her, but reputedly promised to murder Charilaus if he did. Lycurgus, appalled by her vile offer, contemptuously refused her and thus earned her enmity. And notwithstanding the fact that Lycurgus was loved for his honesty and integrity by the people, the evil widow and her family began maliciously to question his motives and ambitions, which so distressed him that he left Sparta and went on a 'Grand Tour', first to Crete, where he studied the laws introduced by Minos, and afterwards to Egypt and possibly then to the Middle East and India.

Soon, however, the Spartans, who were worried about the worsening state of their kingdom, begged Lycurgus to return and become regent until his nephew came of age. Lycurgus said that he would on condition that they let him change the constitution, and upon receiving an assurance to this effect, he went to Delphi to inquire of the god Apollo if he would make good laws, to which the Pythia replied: 'Apollo has heard your request, and promises that the constitution you will establish will be the best in the world.'

Returning to Sparta in 898 BC and becoming co-ruler at age 42 with Archelaus, Lycurgus knew that something radical had to be done about the dual kingship, which had never worked well, owing to the tendency of the two monarchs to argue and disagree, and to become too arrogant and autocratic. Lycurgus therefore made another approach to the Delphic god, who, when asked by him what he should do, succinctly replied:

142

'When you have built a temple to the Syllanian Zeus, and the Syllanian Athene, divided the people into tribes and classes, and established a senate of thirty persons, including the two kings, you shall sometimes invite the people to an assembly between Babyce and Cnacion, and they shall have the determining voice.'

Lycurgus grasped that by creating a senate of twenty-eight responsible citizens along with the two kings, it would act as a balance between the monarchs and the people, controlling the disagreements and autocracy of the former, and the populist excesses of the latter. And by holding outdoor meetings between the river (Cnacion) and the bridge (Babyce), it would effectively concentrate the minds of everybody on what was being discussed. The god's suggestion was therefore put into practice as soon as Lycurgus returned to Sparta, although the people were given no right to propose matters for debate, but could only ratify or reject what was recommended to them by the kings and the senators.

Other changes were implemented to root out insolence, envy, avarice and luxury, the most important of which was the division of available land into equal lots capable of providing the families that worked them with 70 bushels of grain and sufficient wine and olive oil per year. Each family therefore had the same basic rations. The currency was also changed from gold and silver to iron, which was given small value, so that a great deal was required to buy relatively little. This effectively eradicated robbery, for nobody had anywhere to hide large masses of stolen iron nor the carts to transport it, and because iron was virtually valueless to foreigners, it prevented the importation of luxury goods and dissuaded prostitutes, fortune-tellers, sophists, thieves and other outside ne'er-do-wells from visiting Sparta. Similarly, cooking at home was forbidden, so that the citizens ate together at public tables.

Spartan boys, who were all destined to become warriors, were thereafter only taught basic literary and numeracy skills. 'All the rest of their education,' says Plutarch, 'was calculated to make them subject to command, to endure labour, to fight and conquer.' Regular exercise and a moderate diet made them strong and fit, and their behaviour was closely monitored by their parents and guardians, to ensure good manners, respect for others, especially the aged, and a love of their city. In speech they were expected to express themselves in a few, plain words, interlaced with droll humour. There were no foul-mouthed yobs in ancient Sparta and no lewdness or debauchery. And neither was there, thanks to Apollo, any football.

When Charilaus reached his majority, Lycurgus, upon obtaining an oath from the citizens that they would obey 'his' laws without question until his return, left Sparta. He then went to Delphi to inquire of Apollo if the changes he had made were acceptable to him. The god replied, 'The laws are excellent, and if the city keeps to the constitution it will be the most glorious in the world.' Lycurgus wrote the answer down and sent it to Sparta. Having done that, and wishing to hold the Spartans to their oath, he killed himself.

The constitutional changes thus introduced made Sparta into an inward-looking, stable society, whose hardy citizens were satisfied with the basics of life and who shunned luxury and excess. As soldiers they became the most effective fighters in Greece, universally admired for their discipline, courage and bravery. And the laws of Apollo were followed almost without change for 450 years, until gold and silver were allowed into Sparta during the reign of King Agis. Such a development, as Lycurgus had feared, sowed the seeds of her eventual decline. Then in 431 BC she began a war with Athens which lasted for twenty-seven years, for although Sparta was the ultimate victor, the conflict exhausted her citizens, and fatally exposed them to corrupting foreign influences and to wealth and luxury. Thus are those punished who disobey the gods. But the gold of Spartan character had already become earlier tarnished by the acquisition of slaves known as Helots, taken from the Laconian town of Helos, who were treated with great cruelty and contempt.

About 170 years after Apollo assisted Lycurgus in changing the Spartan constitution, a Roman king named Numa also reputedly received a number of god-given laws. Rome had been founded by the twins Romulus and Remus on 21 April 753 BC, and it was ruled by Romulus for the following thirty-seven years, although for part of this period he shared power with Tatius Titus, the Sabine king of nearby Cures.

When Romulus mysteriously vanished on 7 July 714 BC, there followed a short interregnum lasting about one year, at the end of which Numa Pompilius, a Sabine, was elected by the citizens of Rome to succeed him. Numa had been born on the same day as Rome's foundation, which may have suggested a linked destiny with the city, although it was his stalwart, honest character, and his love of justice, philosophy and religion, that marked him out as a suitable monarch. Indeed, Numa's manner and bearing had so impressed Tatius, that he gave him his daughter Tatia in marriage.

Numa and Tatia's marriage lasted until her death thirteen years later. Numa was devastated by her loss, and spent many weeks afterwards wandering alone through the sacred groves near Cures, his native city. It was during this period that he was spoken to by the nymph Egeria, although she may also have appeared to him. He claimed later also to have talked with the Muses, to whom, says Plutarch, 'he ascribed most of his revelations'. Thus it would seem that Numa received from both these divine sources the system of laws with which he is credited and which he introduced to Rome.

When Numa, at age 40, finally accepted the kingship of Rome, he took immediate steps to reduce the aggression and love of warfare of its citizens, who then lived, like the Highland Scots of a later date, by pillage and rapine. To encourage them to follow a more settled and peaceful life, he divided up the surrounding land amongst them and introduced the arts of agriculture and husbandry. This kept the citizens gainfully occupied and enabled them to become self-sufficient in food, while at the same time tying them to the land and to the cycle of seasons. And to unite further the

Romans and the Sabines within a more stable, work-orientated society, he also introduced various trades, like masonry, tanning, weaving, smithery, baking, potting, acting, and musicianship. The development of such skills and the satisfaction they gave, along with the utility or entertainment value of the products, helped give those concerned a vested interest in a settled way of life.

Numa likewise reawakened awe in, and respect for, the gods by forbidding them to be physically portrayed as statues, so that their majesty and might would be felt inwardly, and he also, by outlawing animal sacrifice, separated divine worship from blood, suffering and death. The deities had thereafter to be given offerings of flowers, fruits or vegetables, which were grown and cultivated by the worshipper and were therefore presented as true gifts. Numa also introduced new religious festivals, in which the citizens all took part together.

These and other radical changes made by Numa at the instigation of Egeria and the Muses, were highly successful. During his reign, which lasted, like Hammurabi's, for an astonishing forty-three years, he was not only loved and respected by all his subjects, but Rome enjoyed her longest period of uninterrupted peace. He died after a slow decline, an old man in his early eighties, and he was universally mourned. Plutarch says of him in *Lives*:

It must be acknowledged something truly great and divine in Numa, to be invited from another country to the throne; to make so many alterations by means of persuasion only; to reign undisturbed over a city not yet united in itself, without the use of armed force (which Lycurgus was obliged to have recourse to, when he availed himself of the aid of the nobility against the commons), and, by his wisdom and justice alone, to conciliate and combine all his subjects in peace.

Indeed, no other Roman king or emperor deserves to be remembered as much as he does.

These five early cases of divine contact are important

because the laws that were given by the deities concerned had a formative and lasting effect on the societies which benefited from them. Indeed, I have already mentioned how the Ten Commandments imparted by Jehovah form the basis of our present-day Western morality and indeed of Christianity. And the laws given by the other deities have much in common with these, for they all defined what was socially permissible behaviour and what was not, and laid down various punishments for those who misbehaved.

But while the reader may be willing to accept that Jehovah, who is generally regarded as the one and only God, actually did speak to Moses, he or she will perhaps object to believing in the reality of the other deities. After all, Hammurabi was supposedly spoken to by Shamash, Minos and Rhadamanthus by Zeus, Lycurgus by Apollo, and Numa by a nymph named Egeria and by the Muses. Such scepticism will prompt most to suppose that the five kings either lied about hearing a deity speak or that they were subject to vocal hallucinations.

Yet why should Moses' experience be any more valid than theirs? To say that Moses really heard the voice of God but the others were either lying or imagining things is biased and unfair. None of the kings concerned, who were all exceptional individuals, had any reason to pretend that a god spoke to them, and there is nothing in the historical records to suggest that the voices they heard were hallucinatory. Their own subjects certainly did not think them mad, and neither did they, as far as we can tell at this late date, show any signs of being mentally unstable, unlike many Roman emperors. Moreover, those who followed them were not only their inferiors in every respect, but they all displayed the classic symptoms of mental ill-health, being violent, cruel, greedy, paranoid, and overly ambitious, and all brought suffering to their subjects and disaster to their realms. Yet none of them heard a disembodied voice!

However, while modern Jews believe that there is only one God, namely Jehovah, monotheism was not accepted by all Jews in the days of Moses. Indeed, Moses' father-in-law

Jethro thought that Jehovah was simply the most powerful god, commenting to Moses: 'Now I know that the Lord *is* greater than all gods: for in the thing wherein they dealt proudly *he was* above them' (*Exodus* XVIII, 11). And even Jehovah himself, when giving Moses the Ten Commandments, did not say that He is the only god, but rather confusingly orders, 'Thou shalt have no other gods before me.' Likewise, if Jehovah is the only God, why did he angrily tell Moses that 'I the Lord thy God am a jealous God, visiting the iniquity of the fathers upon the children unto the third and fourth generations that taketh his name in vain'? What did He have to be jealous about if there are no other gods?

Early Christians, while paying lip-service to the idea of monotheism, were too influenced by Greek polytheistic beliefs to jettison them entirely. Thus to Christians God does not exist on his own but as a trinity of Father, Son and Holy Ghost. Jesus Himself was fathered in a similar way to Minos and his two brothers, who are the sons of Zeus and Europa, by God impregnating Mary. And after her death, Mary was deified as the Mother of God. God also has numerous spiritual helpers called angels to whom prayers can be addressed, while righteous churchmen, particularly if they have been martyred, become sanctified after death and thereafter behave in their spiritual form like demi-gods, bringing about miraculous cures, answering prayers and making surprise disembodied announcements. And these divinities, moreover, supposedly exist along with Beelzebub, Lucifer, and Satan, and the rest of the demonic horde.

However, where Shamash, Apollo and Zeus are concerned, it is not necessary to decide if they are separate, individual deities. All three were associated with law-making by their worshippers, hence it is only natural that those seeking legal guidance or assistance would visit their temples or shrines. And clearly, if Hammurabi heard a voice speak to him on the summit of Shamash's ziqqurat, then he would obviously assume that it belonged to the god. The same may be said of the voice heard by Rhadamanthus and Minos at the Dictaen cave: they would have thought that it was Zeus's voice, to whom the cave was sacred. And the voice which spoke to the Pythia was obviously that of Apollo, because the temple was dedicated to him. Thus none of these deities identified themselves: their identity was simply assumed.

Numa was spoken to by Egeria and by the Muses, who were all minor deities, like Christian angels. They probably did not reveal their names, but when Numa heard different voices speaking to him, he doubtless managed to work out, or so he thought, who they were. Besides, the nymph Egeria was traditionally associated with the groves near Cures where he walked, and the Muses, the daughters of Jupiter and Mnemosyne, of whom there were then three, Melete, Mneme, and Aoide, would have given themselves away by speaking of the arts in addition to law.

This perhaps brings us back to the mystical revelations of Nicholas of Cusa and many others, which show that the One is many and the many are One. They suggest that the divinity of God, within which we all reside, can manifest in a variety of ways and forms, which while seemingly dissimilar, and to which we may give different names and identities, are all none the less different aspects of Himself.

While Elijah is reported in *1 Kings* as having heard 'a still small voice' when God spoke to him, there are unfortunately no records of what the divine voice that addressed the other above-mentioned individuals sounded like. Yet there are some later accounts of its tone and quality, although these relate some puzzling, but perhaps now understandable, differences. For unlike the 'small still voice' heard by Elijah, Gregory of Tours (*c.* 540–594) says in his *Historia sive Annales Francorum* that when Saint Salvius clinically died and was taken with others to 'a place that we had already seen from afar and above which was suspended a cloud brighter than all light', he heard 'a voice resembling the sound of mighty waters' emerge from the cloud, that somewhat regally declaimed, 'He may return to earth, for he is necessary to the churches.' A more expected description of God's voice was given by a woman interviewed by Dr Raymond Moody, who stated that when she was brought to the point of death by a serious illness, 'I heard God's voice talking to me. He had the most loving gentle voice . . . it was so overwhelming. He told me that if I wanted to live, I was going to have to breathe . . . and so I did.' This accords with the 'kind, gentle voice' heard by the American GI mentioned in Chapter Three.

However, the divine voice does not usually impart laws, but instead it typically gives a brief order or instruction. I have noted two instances of such disembodied direction in the above paragraph, and more cases are examined in the next chapter. We shall in fact discover how these divine commands have profoundly altered the lives of the people concerned and have thereby helped to change both society and history.

8 The Divine Director

In reality, there are many little circumstances too often omitted by injudicious historians, from which events of the utmost importance arise. The world may, indeed, be considered as a vast machine, in which the great wheels are originally set in motion by those which are very minute, and almost imperceptible to any but the strongest eyes.

From *Tom Jones* by Henry Fielding (1749)

I have already mentioned three Christian saints who were instructed to act in a certain way by a disembodied voice, the trio being Polycarp, Augustine and Margaret of Cortona. The most important of them from an historical point of view is St Augustine (AD 354–430), the greatest early church father, whose masterwork *Concerning the City of God against the Pagans* portrays Christian belief as a holy edifice built on the rubble of a collapsing and depraved pagan Roman empire. Indeed, Augustine's writings helped spread the new religion's message of brotherly love, peace, and everlasting life, while exposing the vanities and temptations of the world, to which we all are subject, as traps and snares laid by the Devil. In fact the child-like disembodied command '*Tolle, lege*' or 'Take it, read it', which brought about the hearer's bibliomanic perusal of a passage from St Paul's *Epistle to the Romans* not only converted Augustine but in turn directed his formidable energy and talents into championing Christianity at a time when it was threatened by imperial apostates and by heretical schisms.

However, the most singular and historically important disembodied voice was that of Jesus, which purportedly spoke to one Saul on the road to Damascus about two years after His crucifixion, in AD 35. Saul, a native of Tarsus and a young man at the time, was a conservative Jew, who hated the Jewish disciples of Christ, whom he regarded as yet another false Messiah, and who therefore, at the behest of the high priests in Jerusalem, actively sought them out in order to have them punished by imprisonment or by death for their religious treachery.

But while travelling with his men to Damascus, where he intended rounding up Jesus's followers and bringing them forcibly back to Jerusalem, Saul and the rest of his party were suddenly bathed in a bright heavenly light, from which a disembodied voice demanded, 'Saul, Saul, why are you persecuting me?' To which Saul, falling on his knees in fright but without knowing who or what was addressing him, replied, 'Who are you, Lord?'

The voice returned, 'I am Jesus, whom you persecute,' adding: 'it is hurtful to you to fight against the inevitable.'

And Saul, trembling violently, asked: 'But Lord, what do you want me to do?' To which the voice answered, 'Get up and go into the city, and there you will be told what to do next.'

The experience then abruptly ended, leaving Saul completely, although temporarily, blind, whereupon he was guided into Damascus by his men, who had also heard the remarkable voice. Their awareness of the event reveals that the voice was not, as some commentators have suggested, an hallucination arising from Saul's subconscious sense of guilt and shame at the persecution of his fellow Jews, but was in fact a genuine external phenomenon, wherein it was similar to the other disembodied voices of dead, if not resurrected, people that I have earlier considered.

However, the voice, while characteristically brief, is unusual in that it first asked Saul a rhetorical question, next identified itself as belonging to Jesus and told Saul that he was only hurting himself by his actions, and then ordered him to proceed to Damascus, where in fact he was going anyway. And once there, the voice added, he would receive further instructions.

While the conversation between Saul and the voice probably took place in less than a minute, it was none the less the most important verbal exchange in world history, for it effectively led to the creation of a new religion and in so doing marked out the course triumphantly taken by Western civilization.

Saul remained blind for three days until a follower of Christ named Ananias came to him and cured him by placing his hands on his eyes. Strangely, Ananias had also been instructed to do this by the disembodied voice of Jesus, which furthermore told him where Saul was staying. And just as importantly, the voice informed Ananias that Saul was 'a chosen vessel' and had been selected to bear his name to the Gentiles and kings, as well as to the children of Israel. Then, following the miraculous restoration of his sight, Saul was baptized and soon afterwards – to everyone's absolute astonishment – he began preaching that Jesus was the Son of God and thus the Messiah.

After adopting the 'Christian name' of Paul, the new disciple remained in Judaea for several years, proclaiming Christ's message to his fellow Jews and thereby incurring the wrath of the Temple priests, but without making much progress except in the sense of learning how to proselytize. But then, probably in AD 45, he left Judaea and first went, with Barnabas and others, to the Syrian city of Antioch, where he preached to both Jews and Gentiles.

As Paul travelled on from city to city, he found that he had most success in converting the Gentiles, who were mainly pagan Greeks, and thereby establishing among them enthusiastic, self-perpetuating groups of believers, who by worshipping together and by communicating one with another, formed the basis of the Christian Church. Indeed, Paul was a tireless traveller and indefatigable evangelist, who almost single-handedly changed a small-time Judaean movement –

and one of many – led by a healer named Jesus (or Yeshu), who had taught that the Kingdom of God could be achieved here on earth by eschewing wealth and by living lovingly with one's fellows, into something that ironically transcended anything that He had hoped for or desired – a new religion which had Him as a God-created Saviour at its centre, and who was crucified, buried and resurrected that we all might live.

Yet the growth of Christianity from a fringe Middle Eastern cult into the spiritual conqueror of the Roman Empire required more than energy and enthusiasm. It also needed official sanction and support at the highest levels of government, or otherwise it would have remained just one of the several competing religions, like Mithraism and Zoroastrianism, which promised a better life in both this world and the next to their adherents. Christians, moreover, were ironically disadvantaged by the fact that many pagans interpreted their certainty of knowing God's Truth as religious arrogance, and who, by refusing to recognize the ancient gods or to pay homage to the genius of the Emperor, brought abuse and repeated outbreaks of persecution down upon themselves.

However, Christianity finally gained the required imperial approval and support at the beginning of the fourth century AD. This happened, amazingly enough, as a direct result of another supernatural experience, one similar to St Paul's. The witness of the event was none other than Constantine, later surnamed 'the Great', who, although he did not hear a disembodied voice, did see its visual equivalent in the form of a written message in the sky. The unexpected celestial instruction not only helped bring about Constantine's victory over his foes, but it converted him to Christianity. His conversion was the second giant step taken by the faith, for it brought Christianity on to the centre stage of both religious and, more importantly, political life.

Constantine, the son of Constantius and his concubine Helena, was born in what is now Serbia in AD 274. Having made a career for himself in the army, he accompanied his father, who then ruled as co-emperor with Galerius, to Britain in early AD 306 to help repel an invasion by the Picts. But Constantius, after achieving a magnificent victory over the northern barbarians, unexpectedly died at York on 25 July, whereupon his son was immediately declared Emperor in his place by the troops.

Constantius had been generally favourable to Christianity, whereas Galerius, like the former joint emperors Diocletian and Maximian, was hostile to it and he violently persecuted its followers from his accession to the purple in AD 305. Constantine followed his father's inclinations, however, and viewed Christians with bemused tolerance. Yet his equivocal attitude was changed dramatically in AD 311, when, following the death of Galerius, he was obliged to take arms against Maxentius, the ambitious son of Diocletian's former co-emperor Maximian. For soon afterwards, when he was still in Gaul, the above-mentioned supernatural display occurred. John Crevier describes it thus:

Constantine, as he was marching with his army, towards evening, when the day began to decline, saw, in the sky, just over the sun, the figure of a luminous cross, with this inscription, 'By this thou shalt conquer' [In hoc signio vinces]. His army saw, as well as himself, this miraculous phenomenon, which struck all the beholders with great astonishment. Constantine, though he lived in the midst of Christians, and was extremely kind to them, had so little notion of Christianity, that he did not know the meaning of the cross. A dream informed him of it. In the night, Jesus Christ appeared to him with his cross, and commanded him to have a representation made of that which he saw, and to use it in all his battles as a sure defence against his enemies.

The following morning Constantine had such a cross made, which became the new *Labarum* or imperial standard around which his army marched. But that was not all, for on reaching Rome in October of AD 312, he had another dream in which he was likewise told to have the Christian *chi-rho* (XP) mono-gram inscribed on his soldiers' swords and shields. The order was carried out and the promise of victory was shortly after-wards fulfilled, for he crushed Maxentius and his army, and thereby made himself undisputed ruler of the Roman empire. His victory was not only the first for a Christian army, but it fully persuaded Constantine that with Jesus Christ he and the Roman people would triumph over the enemies of Rome and live in peace under one God.

In March of the following year (AD 313), Constantine, along with Licinius, his brother-in-law and new co-emperor, issued the famous Edict of Milan, which announced 'that it was right that Christians and all others should have freedom to follow the kind of religion they favoured', and forbade others from troubling or molesting them in any way, and ordered the immediate restoration to them of their holy places, free of charge, by those who had bought the proper-ties. But it is ironic to note that whereas the edict benefited Christians most by promising them freedom of worship, such civilized liberty was soon thrown out of the window by them when they consolidated their hold on the state.

At about the same time that these great events were being enacted in Italy, an Egyptian Christian named Anthony was taking up residence in a cave on Mount Kolzim, situated on the north-west corner of the Red Sea. He was then about sixty years old and he would remain in that remote spot, far from the world of noise, bustle and temptation, until his death in AD 356. Anthony, despite his poverty, was the scion of a wealthy, Christian family, and he had developed a fondness for prayer and meditation while still a child. His parents died when he was about twenty, and not long afterwards, while in church, he was struck to the heart by a verse read from the Gospel of St Matthew, wherein Jesus says to a young rich man: 'If thou wilt be perfect, go and sell that thou hast, and give to the poor, and thou shalt have treasure in heaven: and come and follow me.' Anthony took this scriptural reading as a sign from God, much as Augustine would later do when he read that passage from St Paul's *Epistle to the Romans*, and he resolved to follow its command.

Shortly afterwards Anthony sold his property, gave the proceeds to the poor, and placed his younger sister with some nuns. Then he took up residence in an abandoned house at the edge of his village, situated about sixty-five miles south of Cairo, where he resolved, by means of self-denial and austerity, to make himself pure in body and soul. Later he moved to a tomb in the village cemetery, which stood further away on a nearby mountainside, and from there he went into the desert, where he lived in a cave at Pisir.

But his solitary life was not without attendant difficulties, both mental and physical. The former included regret for past comforts and certainties, as well as anxieties about the future, and the latter, his natural youthful sexual desires. These he grappled with and eventually overcame, but they were soon replaced by a series of awful visions, wherein the Devil, or so he believed, threatened him in the shape of various dangerous animals, argued with him in the semblance of brother monks or dark-skinned Indians, tempted him with phantom piles of gold and silver, and once appeared to him in his own terrifying guise.

Yet Anthony also heard a 'voice from heaven' speak to him on more than one occasion. The first time this happened was after he had seen the above-mentioned diabolical beasts, whereupon the voice of God revealed that He had been with him, that He had watched how he dealt with them, that He would from thenceforth be his guide and comforter, and added 'I will make thee to be renowned as a faithful servant throughout all the earth.' The second time occurred many years later when Anthony, having received several irksome visitors, was considering going into the desert to do some silent contemplation, when a disembodied voice told him that if he did go, he would have less peace than he had already. And this, indeed, proved to be the case. Lastly, and perhaps most interestingly, following a dispute with others about where the soul went at death, the same voice from heaven said to him commandingly a day or so later: 'Anthony, get thee forth, and thou shalt see.' And looking up, he saw the giant form of a grotesque man around whom were walking numerous beings, some of which had wings and could fly, and were thereby rising upwards and out of sight. The grotesque man, Anthony noticed, was 'gnashing his teeth with bitterness' at the sight of those forms which flew out of his reach, and he understood that the figure was Satan and the escaping forms were the souls of dead people who had lived good and righteous lives. They were ascending to heaven; the remainder, however, were trapped by their sins with Satan.

Today such occurrences are dismissed as hallucinations, which were produced in Anthony's mind by solitude, lack of sleep, extreme heat and an inadequate diet, and which together, it is supposed, brought him to the brink of madness. Yet people in those far-off days were familiar with insanity, and nobody thought that Anthony was mad or even eccentric. Indeed, as the years passed and his fame as a desert solitary grew, he attracted hundreds of admiring visitors and disciples, all of whom were struck by his innate dignity, by the gravity and wisdom of his discourse, and by the health and strength of his body. Even the Emperor Constantine and his sons Constantius and Constans knew of him, and all three, having 'heard concerning his works and triumphs ... began to write epistles unto him as a father and to entreat him to pray for them, and they longed greatly to become the recipients of letters from him.' But whereas those with him were thrilled and excited by such imperial correspondence, Anthony remained completely unmoved by it, simply remarking, 'What need is there for wonder, seeing that it is only one man writing letters to another?'

Amazingly, for most of his life Anthony ate only dry bread and salt, drank nothing but water, slept little and on the floor, and never washed, but he none the less lived to be 105 years old. His biographer Athanasius, who knew him well, remarks of him shortly before his death: 'In spite of his great old age. his eyes waxed not dim, and not one of his teeth dropped out, and both his hands and feet were in a sound and healthy state; and notwithstanding that he kept his body low (in respect of food), his appearance was more glorious than that of all those who fed themselves luxuriously on dainty meats, and who wore fine clothes, and who made use of baths. And moreover he possessed strength which was out of all proportion to his aged body.' There is in this, it seems, an example for us all.

Anthony was arguably the first of the Christian desert ascetics who attempted to get closer to God by turning their backs on the world. His example was quickly emulated, and throughout his long life, as mentioned above, increasing numbers of seekers came to him, begging for instruction and guidance. These monks, as they were called, at first lived alone or in pairs, but later Anthony found it convenient to place some together in groups, in a particular dwelling, where they lived, worked and worshipped communally. Hence Anthony not only began the long Christian tradition of individual seclusion, but likewise founded monasticism. Indeed, both hermits and monasteries were common in England up until the sixteenth century, when King Henry VIII, for the sake of a hoped for son, divorced his wife Catherine and broke with Rome, an act which led to the dissolution of the monasteries and to the ending of this ancient, but albeit by then corrupted, way of life.

Unsatisfied sexual desire or lust was the chief antagonist of the solitary desert dweller, and many wrestled constantly with lascivious thoughts and carnal desires, which made it almost impossible for them to uplift their minds to God and to things of the spirit, and which temptation, of course, they blamed on the Devil. The problem, moreover, not only affected the young. One such former victim was an elderly monk named Pachomius, who told a troubled visitor named Palladius, whose own mind was then 'dark and obscured by the thoughts of lust' and who came to him for guidance, that when he was fifty years old 'lust placed itself upon me for twelve years, never going away from me either by night or by day, and I thought in my mind that God had forsaken me.'

159

Unable to find any respite from his raging desires, Pachomius was driven at last to lie one night outside a den of hyenas in the hope that when they came out they would kill and eat him. Yet astonishingly, the hyenas on emerging only sniffed and licked him, but otherwise left him unharmed. Returning disappointed to his cave, the poor man was then assailed by startlingly lifelike visions of a beautiful Ethiopian girl, whom he had once seen in his youth, who seemingly came and sat on his knee and let him play with her parts, and with whom he imagined he had sexual intercourse. But afterwards, despairing of ever freeing himself from such sensual abomination, Pachomius returned to the open desert and searched until he found an asp, which he picked up and held it close to his body, hoping it might bite him and thereby put an end to his awful sufferings.

However, the snake did not bite him; instead, a disembodied voice spoke out, saying: 'Go home, Pachomius, and be strong; I have allowed you to be overcome so that you don't imagine you are a mighty man and a man of perfection, and that you have triumphed through your own life and deeds. You should know that your nature is infirm and feeble and that you cannot rely upon your asceticism, but must always want the help of God and so cry out to Him constantly.' After that somewhat lengthy explanation the curse of lust left Pachomius, never to bother him again. His repetition of the words also brought comfort to Palladius, who left knowing that he had to be strong and mighty in God.

Equally remarkable were the temptations to which Eusebius or St Jerome (AD 342–420) was subject during his four-year stay in the barren desert of Chalcis, situated southeast of Antioch, where it was so hot, he noted, that it 'frightens even the monks that inhabit it.' Eusebius wrote that:

In this exile and prison to which for the fear of Hell I had voluntarily condemned myself, with no other company but scorpions and wild beasts, I many times imagined myself witnessing the dancing of the Roman maidens as if I had been in the midst of them. My face was pallid with fasting, yet my will felt the assaults of desire: in my cold body and in my parched-up flesh, which seemed dead before its death, passion was able to live.

Yet Eusebius was able at last uniquely to overcome his sexual urges by becoming the student of a Jewish monk, who taught him Hebrew, which thankfully delivered him from lustful thoughts. Later, Eusebius became the best-known and most accurate of early church historians.

When the Emperor Theodosius (ruled AD 378–395) needed a tutor for his two sons Arcadius and Honorius, a learned senator named Arsenius, who had been recommended to him by the Pope, was given the job. Arsenius was the boys' tutor for ten years, but his efforts were largely in vain as they were lazy, greedy and intractable, neither having inherited any of their father's exemplary qualities. Indeed, Arsenius became increasingly frustrated by them and bored with the vanity, sycophancy and tedium of life in the imperial household. But then, as if in answer to his prayers and uncertainties, came a divine pronouncement in the form of an advisory disembodied voice, which changed the entire course of his life. It simply said to him, 'Flee the company of men and you shall be saved.'

The command struck a chord with Arsenius, who was by nature a retiring, somewhat solitary man, and as soon as he gained permission from the emperor to leave his employment, he took a vessel from Constantinople to Alexandria in Egypt, from whence he made his way to the desert of Skete, which was the favoured destination for those who wished to retire from the world and find God. There he joined a monastery headed by a father named St John the Dwarf, where he spent the rest of his life in complete poverty, working at making palm leaf mats and baskets, which were sold or exchanged for food and other basic necessities, and enduring long fasts, abstinences and periods of prayer. He eventually became renowned for his sanctity and wisdom, and when once asked why he eschewed the company of his fellows, he replied, 'I find I cannot be both with God and with men at the same

time; nor can I think of leaving God to converse with men.'
When Arsenius was in due course made a saint, he also earned
the sobriquet, which he shared with his former imperial
master Theodosius and indeed with Constantine, of 'the
Great'.

Towards the end of the following century, in about AD 495,
a 15-year-old Italian boy named Benedetto was sent to Rome
by his wealthy parents to complete his education. Benedetto,
however, while clever and eager to study hard, was soon
disgusted by the lewdness and idleness of his schoolfellows.
He therefore left Rome and, wishing to purify himself in the
manner made familar by St Anthony, Pachomius and other
monks, sought refuge in the rocky barrenness of Subiaco,
some forty miles from the city. There he encountered an
elderly hermit named Romano, who, hearing of his troubles
and of his desire for salvation, offered to help him and indeed
fed him on bread from his own meagre rations. Benedetto
took up residence in a nearby cave, where he devoted himself
to prayer and meditation, and to reading the Scriptures.

Three years later, just before Easter, Romano died, but
Benedetto, wholly absorbed in his religious devotions, had no
knowledge of this, nor had he, as the days went by, any awareness of his own need for nourishment. Yet he was saved from
starvation by a local priest, who having prepared a repast for
Easter Sunday, was spoken to in the night by an angelic voice,
which said accusingly to him, 'You have made a banquet for
yourself while my servant on yonder mountain dies for lack
of food.' This supernatural outburst so shocked the priest,
that as soon as the day dawned, he set out with his food to
look for the unknown starving man, and after a long and
desperate search, came across Benedetto as night fell, barely
alive in his lonely cave. Indeed, he did not even know it was
Easter. The two thereupon broke bread and celebrated the
festival together.

Benedetto, or to use his now-familiar Latinized name of
Benedict, remained at Subiaco, and such became his reputation for holiness that increasing numbers of seekers were

attracted there, which eventually led him, like Anthony beforehand, to organize them into monastical groups, wherein they could support and encourage one another. But his greatest contribution to Christian life happened later, following his discovery that pagan rites were being practised on nearby Mount Cassino. To combat these he went to the mountain and founded a monastery, and to regulate the activities of the monks living there, he formulated the now-famous Rule of St Benedict. This includes a number of obligations, of which the need to work manually for seven hours a day and the requirement to take a vow of perpetuity, were added to the familar ones of poverty, chastity, and obedience. The Order of St Benedict, as those following his rule are known, grew swiftly in popularity and became very influential even before its founder's death in 543.

One beneficiary of Benedictine monastical life was an Englishman now known as St Boniface (born c. AD 675), but whom was christened Wynfrid by his wealthy Devon parents. Like Anthony, he felt the call of Christ as a child and he was sent to the Benedictine monastery near Exeter, in order to be educated and trained as a monk. From there he went to the abbey at Nursling, in Hampshire, where he not only studied but taught poetry, history, rhetoric and the Scriptures, as well as composing the first Latin grammar. By such work he became well-known throughout Wessex, to the extent of being consulted by King Ine. Yet when Boniface was about 40 years old he was spoken to by an inner disembodied voice – audible, it was said, though inarticulate (whatever that means!) - as he walked meditatively through the abbey's long corridors or prayed before the crucifix in his cell, which commanded, 'Go and preach the Gospel to all nations'.

Boniface heeded the call, and in 718 he left for the continent, stopping first in Frisia, where pagan invaders had destroyed many of the churches. After visiting the Pope at Rome in 719, he next proceeded into what is now north Germany, to preach Christianity to the heathens and to establish there, at towns like Fritzlar, Amöneburg and Fulda,

Benedictine monasteries for men and cloisters for women. He laboured in this way for thirty-five years, becoming in due course an archbishop, and he was universally loved for his wisdom, learning, and good-humour. But after returning to Frisia, he was martyred by pillaging heathens in 754 at Dokkum, along with fifty-two fellow Christians. St Boniface is still remembered today with gratitude and affection by German and Dutch Christians, although he is largely forgotten in his own country.

A similar divine command was received by a young Italian named Giovanni Bernadone, who, because he had learned French from his wealthy father, was nicknamed 'Il Francesco' or 'the Frenchman', which later became shortened to Francis, the name by which he is known today. Born at Assisi in 1182, Francis grew into a somewhat vain, pleasure-loving boy, whose natural generosity and compassion saved him from becoming arrogant. His golden youth ended, however, when he was captured while fighting for Assisi against neighbouring Perugia, where he was imprisoned for a year. On returning home he caught a serious fever, and was ill for several months, during which time he reflected deeply on the world and his contribution to it, and found himself wanting. When he recovered he met one day an old friend and comrade, who had once been a man of wealth and style, but who was so reduced by poverty that Francis at first did not recognize him. Shocked, Francis exchanged clothes with him, and that night, to his surprise, he had a dream about Jesus. Shortly afterwards he went into the ruined and deserted church of San Damiano to pray, where he heard, while kneeling before a crucifix, a voice say clearly within him: 'Francis, repair my Church, which is falling into ruin.'

This divine instruction was misinterpreted by Francis, who hurriedly bought bricks and mortar in order to repair the San Damiano church, but realized his mistake when his attempt at DIY was laughed at by his fellow citizens, although he later raised money for the restoration of many Assisi churches. He then turned his back on his family and their wealth, and, clad only in a rough cloak and taking nothing with him, he set out to preach Christ's message of charity, repentance, and rejection of the world, to all who would listen. His preaching attracted crowds of excited listeners, several of whom became his disciples, including one woman, Clara d'Assisi. These disciples were united together by the strict rules Francis formulated, the chief of which were complete poverty, chastity and obedience. Later, the Pope, at the urging of a dream wherein he saw the falling walls of the Lateran church in Rome supported by Francis alone, gave sanction to his new order, whose monks are distinguished by their grey or brown habits, tied with cords. And Clara d'Assisi, who left her family to follow Francis when still a beautiful 14-year-old virgin, was later to establish the Poor Clares. Today monks of the Order of St Francis work to relieve the poor, the sick and the suffering throughout the world.

Another virgin who later followed St Francis was Crescentia, of Kaufbeuren in Bavaria, who was born in 1682. When a child, Crescentia had a similar experience to St Francis, for as she humbly knelt before a crucifix in the chapel of the Kaufbeuren convent for Franciscan nuns, she heard a disembodied voice command, 'This shall be your dwelling place.' She soon afterwards joined the convent, but it was only after enduring many years of hardship and humiliation there from her fellow nuns, who looked down on her, that she was rewarded with glorious visions and raptures, and then, many years after her death in 1744, with beatification.

The apparent garrulity of some crucifixes and other church statues, or rather that of the disembodied voices which spoke near or through them, is amusingly described by François Mission (1650?–1722), a French Protestant, in his *A New Voyage to Italy*. He wrote:

You have heard of the Crucifix at St Paul's [i.e. in Rome], which spoke to St Bridget; but you must know that it is not the only Image that has learned to prattle. Another Crucifix at St Maria Transpontina has discoursed several Times with St Peter and St

Paul: And our Lady of St Cosme and St Damian chid St Gregory very sharply for passing by without saluting her. Besides, I know two others at St Mary the Empress, and at St Gregory's on Mount Celio, whose Tongues upon Occasion have wagged very briskly: and how many more, whom I do not know?

As we have noted, the occasions when a divine voice is heard giving a command vary quite a lot, although few instances can be quite so singular as that which attended the one heard by a French boy named Bénezet. One day, when he was looking after his mother's sheep in the Ardennes there was a solar eclipse, and during the strange darkness he heard his name called thrice, followed by the order, 'Build me a bridge over the river at Avignon!' And although Bénezet was young, poverty-stricken and knew nothing about bridge building, he did eventually manage, through persistence and strenuous application, to begin the construction of that much needed bridge, which was completed four years later after his death in 1184.

A 15-year-old Parma girl named Ursulina also heard a disembodied voice speak to her several times about something awful at Avignon, although it was not referring to the town's lack of bridges, but rather to its alternative pontiff, Clement VII, who resided there. In this dramatic way she was instructed to go to Avignon and persuade Clement to renounce his claim to the papacy in favour of Urban VI at Rome. But despite the divine order and after making two arduous journeys on foot from north Italy to Avignon, Ursulina's pleas to Clement fell on deaf ears, for he refused to vacate the second papal throne.

The most famous female recipient of disembodied voices was Joan of Arc, the daughter of a French peasant, who was born in 1412 at Domrémy, in eastern France. Her childhood and youth were evidently happy, if restricted by the conventions of the time, and she was used to hard farm work. Joan became, however, very pious and God-fearing, and she developed a dislike of the English, who controlled the neighbouring region of Burgundy and who sometimes mounted cross border raids. But while Joan's story is full of interest and she played a major part in driving *les Anglais vaillants* from French shores, following the instructions of her heavenly voices – 'Everything that I have done that was good I did by command of my voices,' she later said – the number and frequency of these, and the fact that they were generally uttered by visionary saintly figures (whom she called her Counsellors), effectively discounts their inclusion in this volume. Yet we can quote a description, taken from the *Procès de condamnation*, of the first voice that spoke to her, at age 13, and which, like that heard by Saul and his companions on the road to Damascus, appeared in a divine light.

And on that first occasion she was much afraid. And this voice came to her about the hour of midday, in the summertime, in her father's garden. . . . She heard the voice upon the right side, towards the church, and she rarely heard it without an accompanying brightness. . . . And, after she had heard this voice upon three occasions, she understood that it was the voice of an angel.

The voice was therefore similar to many of those we have earlier considered, in that it spoke without warning, it was heard when Joan was out of doors, and it was neither recognizable nor did it announce its identity. It was only later that she 'understood' it was that of an angel.

Also historically important was the voice heard by George Fox, the founder of the Society of Friends, otherwise known as the Quakers, so-called from their habit of physically trembling whenever they became embued with the power of the Lord.

Born in July, 1624, at Fenny Drayton, Leicestershire, George Fox was a naturally solemn and religious child, who was in due course apprenticed to a shoemaker in Nottingham. However, the direction of his life changed dramatically when, on visiting a fair at age nineteen, he was invited for a drink by two religious professors, one of whom was his cousin

Bradford, who both thoroughly shocked him by drinking more than was good for them.

Later that day, when at home and pacing his bedroom floor unable to sleep, he heard (as he believed) God's voice say to him: 'Thou seest how young people go together into vanity, and old people into the earth; thou must forsake all, both young and old, and keep out of all, and be as a stranger unto all.' Obedient to this command, which was similar, as we have noted, to the vocal directives given to many hermits of old, Fox left home on Saturday, 9 September 1643. He headed south on foot, keeping to himself but suffering none the less all sorts of doubts and anxieties, until at last he reached London, where he had an uncle, but found that 'all was dark and under the chain of darkness', much like the capital still is today.

However, Fox soon bent his steps back home, where he stayed for one year, making frequent visits to local 'steeple houses', as he called churches, and arguing about religion with their parsons. Indeed, he often took it upon himself to interrupt services, which sometimes led to him getting beaten up for his pains, although once, when he entered a church in Mansfield (in 1647), God's voice said to him, 'That which people trample upon must be thy food.'

Fox began holding his own services, usually outside or in barns, and he became another man while preaching at them, 'wrapped up, as in a rapture, in the Lord's power'. His spellbound listeners frequently became his followers or Friends, transformed by the marvellous sense of divinity which had surged through them, making them quake. Some were in turn inspired to preach, which often brought abuse, beatings and imprisonment, as Fox experienced, for not everyone liked their criticisms of the established church or their claims to be in direct communication with the Lord. Yet at their own prayer meetings Quakers sat silently, believing that God, who existed within them, would fill them with His presence and speak with them, much as He did with their founder. This sometimes happened unexpectedly elsewhere, and Fox records in his *Journal* that in 1650 he was visited in prison by a Parliamentary trooper, who had been sent to him for guidance by God's command. The trooper, it seems, had heard a divine voice say to him as he sat in church, 'Dost thou not know that my servant is in prison? Go to him for direction.'

As the Quakers grew in number they suffered increasing discrimination and persecution, which forced many of them to flee to America, where they founded communities based on their beliefs. One of the most important personages in this regard was William Penn (1644–1718), the son of Admiral Sir William Penn, who had received from King Charles II a large tract of land alongside the Delaware River, in lieu of payment for his services. On being granted at his father's death the power to found a new colony there, William Penn named the territory Pensylvania (later Pennsylvania) in honour of his progenitor, with the purpose of establishing a permanent refuge for his co-religionists there. The following year (in September, 1682) he sailed aboard the *Welcome* for the Delaware River with one hundred Friends, chiefly from his home county of Sussex, in order to put this plan into effect.

On his arrival six weeks later at Newcastle, Penn set about explaining his ideas to earlier immigrants, who were mainly Dutch and Swedish, agreeing the borders of his province with his neighbours in Maryland and elsewhere, and in coming to a fair and just deal with the native Indians, with whom he resolved to live in peace, by open purchase of their land. The famous meeting with the latter was held at Coaquannoc, where Penn was later to found Philadelphia, or the 'City of Brotherly Love'.

In their poem *Penn and the Indians* (1827) celebrating the accord reached between the two races, William and Mary Howitt include the following verse, which mentions the vocal messages that were often received, as I have earlier pointed out, by America's native inhabitants:

> Roaming, in their free lives, by lake and stream;
> Beneath the splendour of their gorgeous sky;

Encamping, while shot down night's starry gleam,
In piny glades, where their forefathers lie;
Voices would come, and breathing whispers seem
To rouse within the life which may not die;
Begetting valorous deeds, and thoughts intense,
And a wild gush of burning eloquence.

Later, Pennsylvania became one of the thirteen original American states and it was to play an important part in the War of Independence. Indeed, it was at Philadelphia that the Declaration of Independence was adopted. And all this came about because 19-year-old George Fox once heard a voice say to him, 'Thou seest how young people go together into vanity, and old people into the earth; thou must forsake all, both young and old, and keep out of all, and be as a stranger unto all.'

In 1764, a 16-year-old girl named Anne Mary Redi, who was being educated at a convent of Benedictine Nuns in Florence, where she had been sent by her wealthy Tuscan family, went into her room one day and suddenly heard a disembodied female voice say to her, 'I wish to have you among my daughters.' The startled teenager then felt herself compelled to go into the convent's chapel, where she knelt before the altar in prayer, only to hear the voice again speak. It said, 'I am Teresa of Jesus, and I tell you that soon you will be in my convent.'

Anne Mary shortly afterwards returned home, but obedient to the voice she renounced the world and entered the convent of St Teresa at Florence in 1765, where she remained for the rest of her short life, taking the names Teresa Margaret. There she passed an exemplary retirement, combining prayer, poverty and penances with charitable work among the poor, which led to her eventual sanctification. Her holiness in life evidently infused her physical body, because when she died in 1770 her corpse failed to decay, and to this day it remains uncorrupted by putrefaction.

Another disembodied summons from the deceased Teresa of Jesus, who is better known as St Teresa of Avila, was coincidentally also heard by a second young woman named Anne Mary, the daughter of a wealthy French farmer surnamed Javouhey. Having resolved to remain celibate and to devote her life to the education of poor children, Anne Mary became a nun at the Sisters of Charity convent at Besançon. While there (probably in 1799) she had an extraordinary vision of a room occupied by black children, and at the same time she heard a disembodied voice say to her, 'These are the children God gives you. I am Teresa, and I will look after your congregation.' In due course, following two years spent in Switzerland, Anne Mary started a school first at Chamblanc, and then at Cluny. At the latter town, having acquired several teaching helpers who were also nuns, she founded an order named the Congregation of St Joseph of Cluny, whose teaching work and other charitable acts were continued when Anne Mary began a school at Paris. It was there that her educational excellence came to the notice of the French governor of a small African island named Réunion, which lies east of Madagascar, who asked for her help in founding a missionary school for the native black population. His request brought about the fulfilment of St Teresa's disembodied message, for Anne Mary was later to devote herself to the education of impoverished blacks in Senegal, Gambia and Sierra Leone in Africa, and in French Guiana and elsewhere in South America. She also argued strongly in favour of the emancipation of slaves, despite encountering much opposition, as well as helping to educate and thus civilize those who had been freed. Anne Mary Javouhey died in 1851, and she was afterwards beatified.

A most interesting modern example of a divine voice whose words had a profound effect on the life of the man who heard them is recounted by the Rt Hon. Sir Brian Mawhinney, MP, the former Secretary of State for Transport and Chairman of the Conservative Party, in his autobiography entitled *In the Firing Line*. Sir Brian says that in 1975, following several unsuccessful attempts to be selected as a Conservative Party candidate, he decided to apply (along with ninety-two

others!) for the vacant Peterborough seat, despite having
already been offered the Northampton North candidacy if he
chose to not to go ahead.

Yet Sir Brian was shortlisted for interview, and one
Saturday in July he went to Peterborough for the first time,
where he spent the morning strolling about the city in order
to get some feeling for the place. His walk eventually brought
him to the cathedral, into which, being a devout Christian, he
was drawn to pray. There Sir Brian told God that he felt some
uncertainty about whether he really wanted to or should
represent Peterborough as its MP, but said that as he only
desired to do as He willed, then would He, if he was doing the
right thing, give him a sense of certitude about it?

After he had prayed, Sir Brian felt the awesome silence of
the cathedral close about him:

Yet in that silence I heard words quite clearly spoken. They were
not audible; they were only in my subconscious spirit, but to me
they were very real. I heard what seemed to be a voice saying,
'This is where I want you to be.' I left the cathedral believing that
my prayer had been answered.

Sir Brian's experience, like those of so many others, was, as he
afterwards remarks, 'a defining moment' in his life, and he left
the cathedral to continue walking around Peterborough 'with
a calmness of spirit which I previously had not possessed'.
And although the voice, which was internally heard and
anonymous, had made no reference to the outcome of the
interview, its brevity of utterance was not only typical, but the
implication of what it said was clear. Sir Brian (or rather Brian
Mawhinney, as he was then) was eventually selected as the
Conservative candidate for Peterborough – helped, he reveals,
by a skilled parody of Harold Wilson! – and just under four
years later, following Callaghan's notorious 'Winter of
Discontent', he was voted into Parliament with a substantial
majority of over 5,000. And he represented the city, where
God seemingly wanted him to be, until just before the 1997

General Election, when boundary changes obliged him to switch seats to neighbouring Cambridgeshire North-West. However, this constituency does include some of suburban Peterborough.

I could quote further examples of such disembodied divine commands and advisory comments, but the above are perhaps sufficient to persuade the reader of the relative frequency of such pronouncements and of their considerable impact on the lives of those who have heard them. They illustrate that the voice sometimes identifies itself, as did that of Jesus and the dead St Teresa, although usually it remains anonymous, being interpreted by the hearer as a 'voice from heaven' or an 'angelic voice', or in some cases, like those of George Fox and Sir Brian Mawhinney, as that of God Himself.

The divine voice, however, is essentially no different from the 'ordinary' unknown disembodied voice which people continue to hear, in that it gives a short message of advice or counsel, whose effect on the individual is significant and life-changing, and through whom their society, and indeed the state of the world, can be changed very much for the better. And we should be grateful that such a phenomenon still happens, notwithstanding the sneers and scorn of the committed materialist, to whom all that is truly beautiful and good, and which is seemingly above and outside ourselves, is a superstitious anathema.

9 The Delight of the Cultured Rose

From the air
a voice speaks
it is not mine
and yet it is.

Haiku by the Author

In the previous pages I have related many cases of disembodied voices heard by ordinary people and have noted that the phenomenon is both of considerable interest and, incredibly enough, of importance. Not only have the lives of numerous individuals been dramatically changed by them, but so too has much of human history.

When a known disembodied voice belongs to a living person, who may be far from the hearer, the event naturally implies a possible bizarre means of communication across the miles. If it belongs, on the other hand, to someone who is dead, it in turn suggests that his or her consciousness has survived the experience. Yet many a disembodied voice is unrecognized, which means that it might have come either from an unknown living person or from someone who is dead, or alternatively, it might have originated from some spiritual source, such as a daimonion (good or evil), a spirit, an angel, or even from God Himself. If any or all of the latter possibilities are true, they reveal we are not in control of our lives to the extent that we like to believe, but are subject to a surprising degree of outside influence and direction.

But do such voices actually come from one or other of the

above-mentioned sources or are they really hallucinations? Most scientists and psychiatrists would of course say that the latter is the true explanation, despite indications to the contrary. We must therefore first examine the nature of sound and hearing to help us determine which hypothesis is more likely.

Our brains obtain information about the world around us by means of our sense organs, the five most important being the eyes, the ears, the nose, the taste buds, and the touch receptors in our skin. We also possess receptors that detect pressure, pain, temperature, and so on. But although we commonly say that we hear with our ears, the actual sound is created in the hearing centres of our brains. Sound in fact does not exist outside ourselves: all that there is are vibrations in the air, the so-called 'sound-waves'. Thus when someone claps his or her hands together, for example, the compression of the air between the two palms produces vibratory waves that radiate outwards through the surrounding air. If these enter a person's ears they travel down each ear canal to strike the membranous ear-drum at its base, causing it to vibrate with a corresponding frequency. Three small articulating bones known as the auditory ossicles link the ear-drum with the inner ear, and carry the vibrations of the ear-drum across the middle ear cavity. The vibration of the third ossicle (the stapes) in turn moves the endolymph within the spiral cochlea of the inner ear, which stimulates the nerve endings it contains to generate electro-chemical impulses. These impulses then travel along the auditory nerves to the hearing centres of the brain. And it is within these that the impulses are interpreted as the sound of hands clapping. This is why the world around us is really a completely silent place.

Similarly, when someone speaks they force air out of their lungs over their vocal chords, which are stretched and expanded in various ways that accord with learned directions from the brain, to create, in conjunction with associated brain-controlled movements of the tongue, cheeks and lips, particular and highly complex vibrations in the air leaving the

175

mouth. If these vibrations then enter another's ears they too give rise to corresponding nerve impulses that are carried to that person's hearing centres, which interpret them as the sounds of speech, that is, as words. If he (or she) can interpret the sounds he creates from these nerve impulses, then he is being addressed by someone who speaks his language or at least one he understands. But if, on the contrary, the impulses fail to produce sounds that can be interpreted, then the speaker is talking in a language he does not know.

The same can equally be said of the other senses. Thus taste, smell, touch and sight are experienced in the brain areas devoted to the interpretation of incoming impulses from the tongue, nose, skin and eyes respectively. We all, in other words, actively create the world around us from whatever signals come to us and to which we are sensitive. There is, in other words, no concrete reality out there: the world as we know it only exists in our minds. And this is also why, as the disembodied voice told Julian Jaynes, we must 'Include the knower in the known', for the known is essentially a construct of the knower. The two do not and cannot exist separately from one another. This of course blurs the border, if indeed there is one, between what is hallucinatory and what is not, because if all our sensations are created in the mind, they are all in this regard hallucinations.

But if a disembodied voice is actually produced in our brains from sound-waves entering our ears, then these must somehow arise at the point from which they come. I have already discussed one way in which this may happen, namely via the medium of the double or döppelganger, which is the separated inner form of a person that can be projected to a distant place. The double has many of the characteristics of the physical body, to the extent that it can move and otherwise manipulate objects, while at the same time remaining, as it often does, invisible. It can also, if it separates along with the consciousness of the person concerned, speak. Such separation usually happens when that person is sleeping, who may later recall the experience as seemingly a dream. The invisible, conscious double can then call out the name of the person into whose presence it has projected or alternatively deliver a short message to him or her, who will hear the voice as a disembodied pronouncement. We noted one distinct example of this in the case of the eighteenth-century Bristol clergyman's wife, whose disembodied voice was heard by her husband and daughter lamenting the death of her other child.

At death the double, then known as a wraith, leaves the body along with the person's consciousness, thereby providing the latter with a familiar boundary and setting in which it can embark on its journey to the next world. But the wraith does not necessarily immediately leave the material realm and it can in fact exist here for varying lengths of time. Its departure seems to be impeded chiefly by its worries or concerns about loved ones who have been left behind. While here it is normally invisible to the living although it can sometimes be seen, and it retains the same quasi-material properties that it had during the life of its physical counterpart. It can thus manipulate material objects and it can also speak. Indeed, the wraith has the same personality and the same awareness of its surroundings as the living person. It is therefore an entity that can produce the disembodied voice of its once living physical counterpart, and so can speak a loved one's name or give him or her a short advisory message or a warning, or occasionally even participate in a lengthy conversation. I have described numerous examples of double separation in my book about the phenomenon.

However, while the projection of a double or a wraith may account for many of the cases of known voices being heard, there are others where this explanation seems unlikely. This is particularly true of those in which the voice belongs to a living but distant person, who is awake and fully conscious at the time. In these cases telepathy is one possible solution to the problem, although as we have seen telepathy normally produces in the 'contactee' an inner feeling that something is wrong or amiss, rather than an external disembodied voice, and besides, how can we account for the voice being heard by others at the scene if he or she is the only one being thought about? Indeed, the fact that the voice, whether known or unknown, can be heard by several people at the same time strongly suggests that it originates from outside of them all. The voice in this respect seems to manifest in the air rather like a bubble bursting, producing sound-waves that reproduce those orally generated by the person concerned and conveying the same call or message.

But while telepathy or 'thought transfer' is probably not the means by which a disembodied voice is heard at a distant point, there is another paranormal faculty of the mind that could produce the necessary movement of air molecules there. This is the direct action of mind on matter known as psychokinesis ('mind-movement') or telekinesis. Psychokinesis is a well-known phenomenon and various experiments have been conducted over the years to demonstrate that our minds can directly affect our material surroundings. This ability is perhaps best known and most dramatically seen in the form of poltergeist activity, which typically centres around a repressed and disturbed adolescent, who is able, albeit usually unconsciously, to cause havoc in his or her surroundings by mentally throwing household objects about, twisting curtains and other fabrics into virtually untieable knots, shifting around heavy furniture, and knocking on walls, despite him or her being in another place at the time. The disturbed psyche of the adolescent is thus somehow able to produce the psychokinetic force capable of doing these destructive things and in this way he (or she) 'pays back' his parents or other family members who have, perhaps unwittingly, caused his mental disquiet. But psychokinetic ability is by no means limited to disturbed adolescents and it is in fact something we all possess, although only a relatively few individual adults, like Uri Geller and the Russian Ninel Kulagina, are able to consciously make use of it.

But clearly, if a disturbed adolescent can upset his mother's heavy sofa or throw around her pots and pans psychokinetically, then we can reasonably suppose that an ordinary person, who has such an ability latent within him, could in a moment of crisis create a disturbance in the air molecules at a distant point to give rise to vibrations or sound-waves that correspond to what he actually thinks and says at the time. And because the concentrative effort of directing this latent force would almost certainly manifest as a short pulse or burst, it perhaps accounts for the brevity of what is usually said.

Psychokinetic movement of the air might also explain the other sounds that sometimes accompany the spoken voice, such as those of her son's crashing motorbike that were heard by writer Marion Law. After all, at the moment of the crash, the young man's mind would have been full of that unpleasant noise (which it indeed created) and it may have become so intimately united with his last desperate call to his mother, that when the psychokinetic burst sent by him manifested in her kitchen 5,000 miles away, the crash sounds went with it and were reproduced by the same means in the air for Mrs Law to hear. Equally, the sensation of the rushing wind she experienced may have been produced by the remaining, but unstructured psychokinetic burst from him. Yet none the less it is difficult to account for other sounds like trumpet blasts and celestial music in general, unless of course they were, upon being created in the minds of the players (if any), psychokinetically directed by them to the place where they are heard.

However, if the unknown external voice comes from a daimonion, an angel, or other spiritual entity, then it is probably produced in the same way as the voice of a double or a wraith – by the direct creation of sound-waves in the air, even though these beings are given short shift by scientists. And although I have never met, to the best of my knowledge, an angel, I know of a man who once did on many occasions. This is the Swedish mathematician, scientist and mystic Emanuel Swedenborg (1688–1772), who had over 1000 sightings of angels, and not only when he was in a trance or similar mystical state, for in *Heaven and Hell* he writes, 'I have been permitted to see them when I was fully awake; when I was in the exercise of every bodily sense, and in a state of clear perception.' Furthermore, he describes their appearance in the following way:

From all my experience, which has now continued for many years, I can declare and solemnly affirm that angels as to form are in every respect men; that they have faces, eyes, ears, body, arms, hands, and feet: that they see, hear, and converse with each other, and, in a word, that they are deficient in nothing that belongs to man except that they are not clothed all over with a material body.

As well as their similarity in bodily appearance to men, albeit in a perfect form, angels and other spirits, according to Swedenborg, also live in, and breathe, a spiritual atmosphere, wherein they 'utter their words by means of breath, as men do theirs'. Hence they can communicate with us directly by speech, when their words, if they remain invisible, will appear to come from out of the air. Indeed, Swedenborg adds, 'Angelic speech consists of distinct words like human speech, and is also uttered by sound and heard by sound; for angels, like men, have mouth, tongue and ears, and also an atmosphere, in which the sound of their speech is articulated.'

The daimonion, genius or guardian angel is perhaps the most vocal of these spiritual beings. Such invisible companions, however, will normally either assist or frustrate us, depending on their type, in subtle ways, by creating thoughts and desires that are beneficial or destructive, leaving us to choose which guidance we accept and follow. Yet sometimes, as we have seen, they actually speak, producing sound-waves as we do, that give rise to a voice that likewise emerges from out of thin air.

The daimonion of Socrates was clearly his good daimonion. It also spoke to him frequently, guiding him in all sorts of situations and also enabling him to give helpful advice to others. We do not know why he was able to hear its voice so readily, but we can perhaps suppose that his mind was naturally more open and attuned to such communication. His evil daimonion, by contrast, was not able to 'get through' to him at all. But obviously, if it had been the predominant influence over him, then he would have become a completely different person and the course of his life would have taken him far from virtue's path.

However, the concept of the evil daimonion, if true, brings us full circle to the negative voices heard by schizophrenics, which modern psychiatrists say are hallucinatory. For if Socrates' mind was naturally open to the voice of his good daimonion, then it may be that whatever mental stresses cause schizophrenia do so by sensitizing the mind of the sufferer (when the voice is heard externally) to the nerve impulses created by the sound-waves spoken by his or her evil daimonion. And we would expect such a malignant entity to take full advantage of its communicative opportunities to frequently mock, insult and vilify, or even to order the suicide of, its unfortunate victim.

The idea of madness being caused by evil spirits is an ancient one, but there are plenty of early reports of how, when a mentally ill person was cured of his affliction, a spirit was actually seen leaving his or her body. The curing by Jesus of 'a man with an evil spirit in him' who abraded Him in the synagogue at Capernaum is a case in point. Jesus ordered the spirit to be quiet and to leave the man, and 'the evil spirit shook the man hard, gave a loud scream, and came out of him' (*Mark I*, 21-26). Such a provoking idea is not invalidated by the use of modern anti-hallucinatory drug treatments, for their curative effect may lie in the ability of the drug to restore the mind of the schizophrenic to its normal resistance to the influence of his or her evil daimonion or indeed to that of other malignant spiritual entities.

Where universal or divine consciousness is concerned, which we may identify with God or the Supreme Being, we have noted that it pervades, and indeed comprises, the whole of matter, space and time, so that there is no place where it is not. Indeed, the concept of place is negated by it, for if it is all-pervading and all-encompassing, then nothing separate exists within it. This profound concept of everything being united with, and at one with, everything else – the 'coincidence of opposites' of Nicholas of Cusa – is also at the heart of Eastern mysticism. Indeed, in his book *The Tao of Physics* Fritjof Capra quotes the Taoist Chuang Tzu:

The 'this' is also 'that'. The 'that' is also 'this'. . . . That the 'that' and the 'this' cease to be opposites is the very essence of Tao. Only this essence, an axis as it were, is the centre of the circle responding to the endless changes.

Such a concept is familiar to particle physicists, who have found that if the rate or direction of spin of a group of subatomic particles is changed, it brings about a corresponding change in similar particles at a distant and seemingly unconnected place. Furthermore, if divine consciousness and what we call matter are coeval, then God can have no difficulty in speaking directly to us, should He so wish, either through the air in which we reside or directly into our minds. And if the speaker and the hearer are the same, then not only are we one with God but both the known and the unknown disembodied voice we may hear is paradoxically also our own.

Lastly, I would like to mention again the advisory disembodied voice which spoke to me all those years ago when I was 19 years of age. The reader will remember that I heard it when returning from a dreary night at the university, when I was feeling very hurt by, and depressed about, my love life. The voice said, referring to the girls who had caused my distress, 'You don't have to fall in love with them!' It told me, in other words, that I could control my feelings where the opposite sex were concerned, that I didn't have to lose my heart so easily, and that I could, if I wished, thereby protect myself from the pains of love.

The unknown invisible speaker whose voice emerged so surprisingly from out of the air above me was therefore perhaps a daimonion, but was what it said good advice?

In some respects, it was not. For following its pronouncement I completely lost touch with my more tender feelings and became, in my twenties, something of a womanizer. From then on, I metaphorically resolved, I would pluck the fruits of love without bothering to spend time in watering and tending the plant, or risk getting my fingers pricked by its thorns. But sex without love, as I eventually discovered, is a joyless thing, and the pursuit of women for their bodies alone an exhausting, dehumanizing activity, which only brings emptiness and a bleakness of spirit. Smelling a vase of roses is sweet, but the pleasure is momentary, and it cannot compare with the fulfilment that a gardener feels who has lovingly grown and nurtured, perhaps with some difficulty and disappointment, one rose.

And that is why I believe the voice came from my good daimonion.

Bibliography

Abercrombie, John, *Inquiries Concerning the Intellectual Powers* (John Murray, 1841)

Attwater, Donald, *A Dictionary of Saints* (Penguin Books, 1975)

Aubrey, John, *Brief Lives* (Book Club Associates, 1983)

Aubrey, John, *Miscellanies Upon Various Subjects* (John Russell Smith, 1857)

Augustine, St, *Confessions* (Penguin Books, 1979)

Bettenson, Henry (ed.), *Documents of the Christian Church* (Oxford University Press, 1943)

Boswell, James, *Journal of a Tour to the Hebrides with Samuel Johnson. LL.D.* (Oxford University Press, 1948)

Boswell, James, *The Life of Samuel Johnson. LL.D.* (Office of the National Illustrated Library, 1851)

Briere de Boismont, Alexander, *On Hallucinations*, translated by Robert T. Hulme (Henry Renshaw, 1859)

Brittain, Vera, *Testament of Friendship* (Virago Press, 1980)

Butler, Alban, *Lives of the Saints* (Burns and Oates, 1956)

Carrington, Hereward, *Psychic Oddities* (Rider and Company, 1952)

Cellini, Benvenuto, *Memoirs*, translated by Anne MacDonell (Everyman's Library, 1925)

Cicero, Marcus Tullius, *On Divination*, translated by Hubert M. Poteat (The University of Chicago Press, 1950)

Clark, Ella Elizabeth, *Indian Legends of Canada* (McClelland and Stewart Limited, 1981)

Creighton, Helen, *Bluenose Ghosts* (The Ryerson Press, 1957)

Crevier, John Baptist Lewis, *The History of the Roman Emperors*, translated by John Mill (F.C. & J. Rivington; T. Edgerton; Scatcherd & Letterman, etc., 1814)

David-Neel, Alexandra, *Magic and Mystery in Tibet* (Unwin Paperbacks, 1984)

Davies, Rodney, *Discover Your Psychic Powers* (The Aquarian Press, 1992)

Duckett, Eleanor, *The Wandering Saints* (Collins, 1959)

Ebbut, M.I., *Ancient Britain* (Chancellor Press, 1995)

Flammarion, Camille, *Death and Its Mystery*, translated by Latrobe Carroll (T. Fisher Unwin Ltd, 1922)

Flammarion, Camille, *The Unknown* (Harper and Brothers, 1900)

Fox, George, *Journal* (Everyman's Library, 1924)

Gentleman's Magazine, various issues

Good News For Modern Man (Canadian Bible Society, 1966)

Goulert, Simon, *Admirable and Memorable Histories Containing the Wonders of Our Time* (George Eld, 1607)

Graves, Robert, *The Greek Myths* (Penguin Books, 1955)

Green, Celia, and McCreery, Charles, *Apparitions* (Hamish Hamilton, 1975)

Happold, F.C., *Mysticism* (Penguin Books, 1963)

Hayes, Renée, *The Seeing Eye, The Seeing I* (Hutchinson & Co. Ltd, 1976)

Herbert of Cherbery, Lord, *The Life of Edward Lord Herbert of Cherbury* (John Ballantyne and Co. & John Murray, 1809)

Herodotus, *The Histories*, translated by Aubrey de Selincourt (Penguin Classics, 1954)

Holy Bible (Oxford University Press, 1876)

James, William, *The Varieties of Religious Experience* (The Fontana Library, 1960)

Jameson, Anna, *Legends of the Monastic Orders* (Longmans, Green, and Co., 1891)

Jaynes, Julian, *The Origin of Consciousness in the Breakdown of the Bicameral Mind* (Houghton Mifflin, 1976)

Jocelin of Brakelond, *Chronicle*, translated by L.C. Johns (Chatto & Windus, 1907)

185

Johns, C.H.W. (trans.), *The Oldest Code of Laws in the World* (T.T. Clark, 1903)

Josephus, Flavius, *The Jewish Wars*, translated by G.A. Williamson, (Penguin Classics, 1976)

Kellock, Harold, *Houdini* (Heinemann, 1928)

Lang, Andrew, *Dreams and Ghosts* (Longmans, Green, and Co., 1899)

Lang, Mrs, *The Book of Saints and Heroes* (Longmans, Green, and Co, 1912)

Livy, *The Early History of Rome*, translated by Aubrey de Selincourt (Penguin Classics, 1960)

Lucretius, *On the Nature of the Universe*, translated by R.E. Latham (Penguin Classics, 1951)

Marshall, Catherine, *A Man Called Peter* (Hodder & Stoughton, 1996)

Mawhinney, Sir Brian, *In the Firing Line* (HarperCollins, 1999)

Moody, Raymond, *Reflections on Life After Life* (Corgi Books, 1977)

Moore, Margaret Gordon, *Things I Can't Explain* (Rider & Co., 1943)

Moore, Margaret Gordon, *Coincidence – ?* (Rider & Co., 1948)

Parish, Edmund, *Hallucinations and Illusions* (Walter Scott, Ltd, 1897)

Pausanias, *Guide to Greece*, vol. 1, translated by Peter Levi (Penguin Classics, 1971)

Plato, *The Last Days of Socrates*, translated by Hugh Tredennick (Penguin Classics, 1961)

Prescott, William H., *The Conquest of Mexico* (George Routledge & Sons, 1901)

Rhine, Louisa E., *Hidden Channels of the Mind* (Victor Gollanz Limited, 1962)

Rhine, Louisa E., *ESP in Life and Lab* (The Macmillan Company, 1967)

Rhine, Louisa E., *The Invisible Picture: A Study of Psychic Experiences* (McFarland & Company, 1981)

Roux, George, *Ancient Iraq* (George Allen & Unwin Ltd, 1964)

Sandys, George, *Sandys Travells, Containing an History of the Original and present State of the Turkish Empire* (Printed for Rob Clavel, Tho. Passinger, etc., 1670)

Schamoni, Wilhelm, *The Face of the Saints*, translated by Anne Fremantle (Sheed & Ward, 1948)

Starbuck, Edwin Diller, PhD, *The Psychology of Religion* (Walter Scott, Ltd, 1899)

Swedenborg, Emanuel, *Heaven and Hell* (Swedenborg Society, 1937)

Toland, John, *Adolf Hitler* (Ballantine Books, 1977)

Tyrrell, G.N.M., *The Personality of Man* (Pelican Books, 1948)

William of Newburgh, *Historia Rerum Angliarum*, translated by the Revd Joseph Stevenson, M.A., (*The Church Historians of England*, vol. IV, part II, Seeleys, 1856)

Xenophon, *The Memorable Things of Socrates*, translated by E. Bysshe (G. Sawbridge, 1712)

Index